'HOW TO'

BOOK OF
FLOWER
GARDENING
ANN BONAR

BLANDFORD PRESS

'HOW TO'

The **'HOW TO'** Book of Flower Gardening has been written, designed and illustrated to make simple, clear and satisfying the methods of growing flowering plants and the processes of designing and planning a garden.

BANSHA PROTESIA

Contents

The 'How To' Book of Flower Gardening
was conceived, edited and designed by
Simon Jennings and Company Limited
42 Maiden Lane, London WC2, England

Conceived & Designed by Simon Jennings

Text: Ann Bonar BSc. Hort. MJI.

General Editor: Michael Bowers

Designer & Researcher: Caroline Courtney

Illustrations: Lindsay Blow, Susan Milne

Special Photography: John Couzins

First published in the United Kingdom 1982
By Blandford Press
Copyright © 1982 Blandford Books Limited

American edition:
Edited by Dr. Gilbert S. Daniels
President of the American Horticultural Society
Distributed in the United States by:
Sterling Publishing Co., Inc.
Two Park Avenue, New York N.Y. 10016

Distributed in Canada by:
Oak Tree Press Limited
c/o Canadian Manda Group
215 Lakeshore Boulevard East
Toronto, Ontario, Canada

Text and Illustrations
Copyright © 1981 Simon Jennings & Co. Ltd.

0-7137-1289-9

Printed in Singapore

THE AUTHOR
Ann Bonar is a gardening
writer, journalist, and
practicing gardener. Her
career has included
advisory work for fruit
farmers, garden
consultancy, lecturing in
horticulture and five years
editing gardening books.
Plant hunting in many
European countries has
given her a considerable
knowledge of plants in their
natural settings, and she is
the author of several books
on gardening subjects. Her
titles in the 'How To' series
include: *Basic Gardening,
Vegetable Gardening and
Herbs and Herb
Gardening.*

Introduction

Gardens nowadays are largely devoted to flowering plants. A thousand years ago the lucky owner of a piece of land used it to grow medicinal herbs and a few edible crops to help himself and his family survive. Modern life is not quite so basic, and most twentieth-century gardens consist of ornamental plants.

Within the different groups, plants are chosen almost completely because of their flowers, and the color of these flowers. It is color which primarily influences the ornamental gardener's decisions, whether of flower, leaf or berry but, because leaves are generally green and berries red, and flowers can be any color of the rainbow, it is flowers which have the most influence in choice.

Flower gardening is one of the easiest aspects of gardening. Ornamental plants do not have anything like the number of pests and diseases invading them that vegetables and fruit do. Although many plants grow and flower much better in soil which is moist and fertile, there is a sizeable group which actually need dryish soil, short of plant foods.

Many flowering plants are perennial, shrubs and herbaceous kinds for example, and do not need intensive care the year round. Once planted, they need not be fussed over, unlike many vegetables, which require almost daily attention.

Moreover, the flower garden contributes a great deal towards maintaining a natural environment. Birds, insects, small mammals, soil organisms, even water creatures, all thrive in a garden with a wide variety of flowers.

The flower garden provides a green 'lung' outside many, many buildings. At present, this is a pleasant accessory, but it may well become a necessity.

The purpose of flowers

Flower gardening is open to the widest possible variety of interpretations. The possibilities are endless. But, whether you grow flowers for color, scent, form (or all three), whether you grow them for botanical, commercial or idiosyncratic reasons – or simply because you like to have cut flowers in the house, the need for flowers is recognized and felt by everybody.

Gardening takes place under many different conditions: in order to achieve your desired effects with flowers you will have to suit these conditions to the plants you want to grow. The pages that follow deal with a number of normal garden conditions and suggest the kinds of plants that will do well in them. Many of the plants appear again in the list of detailed growing instructions (*page 46 onwards*) which deals with the most universally popular garden flowers.

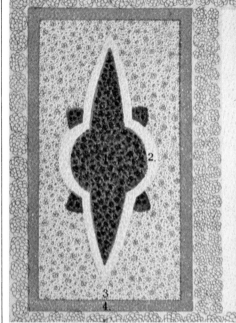

Mesembryanthemum criniflorum

Designing with plants
During the 19th Century, elaborate bedding plans were immensely popular. The design for carpet-bedding at the Crystal Palace, London, *above right,* was one of the more extreme examples. The plants shown, *below right,* are similar to those used in the plans.

6

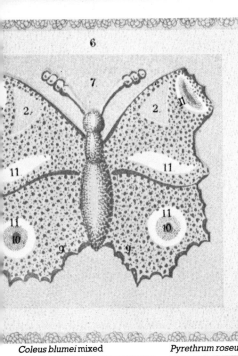

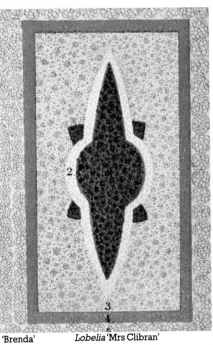

Coleus blumei mixed

Pyrethrum roseum 'Brenda'

Lobelia 'Mrs Clibran'

Basis of choice

If you sit down and think about what sort of garden you want and the kind of plants you want to grow, before you buy them you will have a much more attractive garden than one which is full of 'impulse buys'. These usually prove to be extremely expensive because they are not suited to the garden's aspect and soil, or they turn out to be not what you expected, and take more time to look after than you can spare. You may want a flower garden which requires only the minimum of mainte-

nance. If so, then it will consist mainly of shrubby plants, and low-growing, naturally spreading ground covers so that the minimum of soil is exposed.

You may want a selection of plants that flower in succession so as to provide flowers somewhere in the garden all year round. You may decide to have a massive blaze of color for as long as possible in the growing season, or to specialize, concentrating, for example, on roses, dahlias, or delphiniums.

Perhaps you like to vary the changes

Testing soil
One of the first things to do in your new garden.

Labor saving
Shrubs and paving will cut work down to the minimum.

All year color
This means plenty of work – especially in cool areas.

from year to year, or to grow flowers chiefly for home decoration. Some gardeners prefer formal gardens, tidy, weed-free, well-staked and well-groomed; others like the informal appearance, nearer to the flowery meadows and rock gardens of Nature, in which the plants tumble over one another and flower profusely because they are native to the habitat. Whatever the preferences of you and your family, all considerations must be taken into account before you design and plant.

You should also assess the characteristics of the site: its soil, climate, which way it faces, and so on. Fitting the plant to the site is of the greatest importance; it is the secret of all successful gardening, but especially flower gardening, in which there is such a tremendous choice of plant. This choice may at times seem bewildering, but once you have made a provisional plan and know what sort of garden you want, a number of plants will very quickly suggest themselves as ideal.

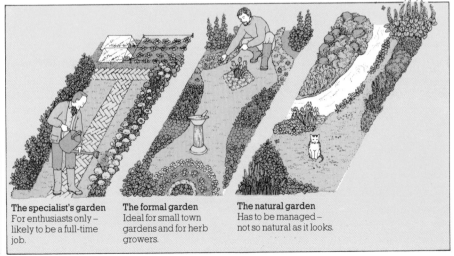

The specialist's garden
For enthusiasts only – likely to be a full-time job.

The formal garden
Ideal for small town gardens and for herb growers.

The natural garden
Has to be managed – not so natural as it looks.

Gardens on clay

Clay soils give you a very wide range of options when it comes to choosing flowering plants. But there are few plants which will tolerate a waterlogged soil, and clay, unless drainage is improved, has a tendency to hold too much water. However, if you follow the advice on soil preparation given overleaf, you should be able to grow most of the flowers dealt with in this book. Shown on this spread is a group of plants well suited to clay soils. Some, like delphiniums, rudbeckia, astilbes and plantain lilies are happy with quite a high degree of moisture in the soil. Others, like phlox, Michaelmas daisies and campanulas prefer well-drained soil. In general, then, you should have no difficulty in growing popular plants of all types in clay soil.

Flowers for clay

1 Delphinium
herbaceous perennial

2 Phlox
herbaceous perennial

3 Michaelmas daisy
herbaceous perennial

4 Sweet pea
annual climber

5 Bergamot
herbaceous perennial

6 Dahlia
tubers/annuals

7 Campanula
herbaceous perennial

8 Plantain lily
herbaceous perennial

9 Rudbeckia
herbaceous perennial

10 Astilbe
herbaceous perennial

Working with clay soil

Heavy soil is always damp or wet, except in prolonged drought. Rain forms puddles on the surface and if a hole a spade deep is dug out during heavy rain, the water will take many hours to drain away from the bottom of the hole.

Clay soils feel sticky when wet, and they crack badly during dry weather. In the spring they remain cold much longer than the medium to light soils.

But a well broken-down clay soil, which has been worked for some years, is fertile and productive, and it is usually deep, with a few stones. Plants grow into much larger specimens than they do on sandy or chalky soils.

Soil improvement

Heavy soil can be structurally improved by the addition of grit or coarse sand dug in before planting, at about 3½ kg per sq m (7 lb per sq yd). Rotted organic matter, such as leafmould, garden compost or farm manure, will also help to get air – and therefore much-needed oxygen – into the soil. It will ensure that water passes through, instead of lingering long enough to get sour. Rates of application can be about 2½-3½ kg per sq m (5-7 lb per sq yd), dug in. A mulch can be 2.5-7.5 cm (1-3 in) thick, depending on the plants; trees and large shrubs will need the larger quantities.

Soil testing

Clay soil can be acid or alkaline. If very acid, lime can be used to reduce it. In winter, allow several weeks between application of lime and that of organic matter. Chalk or ground limestone can be used. If the soil is already alkaline, use gypsum instead, as this has a neutral reaction. Rates of application should be up to 1 kg per sq m (2 lb per sq yd), depending on the degree of acidity. The soil-testing kit will give details.

Plants to avoid

Plants to grow in such soils include all those shown in the corresponding table, and also all those for shady situations, except lilies, camellia, rhododendron and azalea, and witchhazel. Many of those shown in the Chalky Soil group are suitable, except Californian lilac, heather, gypsophila, mullein, musk mallow and scabious. All these need good drainage.

In general, though, you should not experience too much trouble with clay soils, especially if you have improved the drainage and soil structure.

SELECTION OF PLANTS FOR CLAY SOIL CONDITIONS

PLANT	GROUP	COLOR/FLOWERING TIME	HEIGHT/SPREAD
Astilbe	Herb. perennial	Pink, red, white/ early midsummer	23-90 × 30-60cms (9-36 × 12-24ins)
Barberry	Shrub	Orange, yellow/ spring	45-210 × 60-240cms (18-84 × 24-96ins)
Bergamot	Herb. perennial	Red, pink, white/ early summer-fall	60 × 45cms (24 × 18ins)
Bergenia	Herb. perennial	Pink, white, purple/ winter-spring	30 × 45cms (12 × 18ins)
Campanula	Herb. perennial biennial	Blue, white, pink, lavender/summer	30-135 × 30-60cms (12-56 × 12-24ins)
Crabapple	Tree	Red, pink, white/ spring	450-750 × 270-450cms (180-300 × 108-450ins)
Dahlia	Tender tuber	All colors but blue/ summer-fall	23-150 × 23-60cms (9-60 × 9-24ins)
Delphinium	Herb. perennial	Blue, white, lavender, pink, red/summer	75-210 × 30-60cms (30-84 × 12-24ins)
Forsythia	Shrub	Yellow/ early-mid spring	240 × 219cms (96 × 84ins)
Geum	Herb. perennial	Red, yellow, salmon/ spring-fall	30-60 × 30-60cms (12-24 × 12-24ins)
Japonica	Shrub	Vermilion, pink, white/ late winter-spring	75-180 × 120-210cms (30-72 × 48-84ins)
Kerria	Shrub	Yellow/ mid-late spring	210 × 240ins (84-96ins)
Mahonia	Shrub	Yellow/ mid-fall-spring	120 × 150cms (48 × 60ins)
Michaelmas daisy	Herb. perennial	Purple, pink, blue, red, white/fall	15-150 × 60-90cms (6-60 × 24-36ins)
Phlox	Herb. perennial	Pink, purple, white red/ late summer-early fall	90 × 60cms (36-24ins)
Plantain lily	Herb. perennial	White, violet, lilac/ early summer, late summer- fall	30-60 × 45-75cms (12-24 × 18-30)
Rudbeckia	Herb. perennial	Yellow, brown, red/ late summer-fall	60-180 × 60-90cms (24-72 × 24-36ins)
Sweetpea	Climbing annual	All colors/ mid-summer-fall	90-210 × 30-90cms (36-84 × 12-36ins)

Flowers for sandy soils

Very few plants will thrive in poor, starved soils. But, of those shown here, primroses, lavender and milfoil will tolerate conditions of dryness and lack of plant food that would be death to many plants. Nevertheless, all plants would appreciate some enrichment of the soil. If you follow the advice given overleaf, you should be able to grow most of the plants that appear in this book – and many others. This group includes some of the most popular of garden flowers: geranium (cranesbill), border carnations and pinks, gladiolus, lupins and lavender are happy with almost any well-drained soil. Milfoil is a species of *Achillea* and may be better known in some places as yarrow; the one shown here is *Achillea filipendulina*.

The sandy border

1 Senecio greyi
evergreen shrub

2 Milfoil
herbaceous perennial

3 Gladiolus
half-hardy corm

4 Lupin
herbaceous perennial

5 Evening primrose
herbaceous perennial

6 Cranesbill
herbaceous perennial

7 Carnations
herbaceous perennial

8 Pinks
herbaceous perennial

9 Sun rose
herbaceous perennial

10 Lavender
evergreen shrub

Working with sandy soil

The type of soil that feels gritty to the touch when rubbed between thumb and forefinger, or which contains a lot of gravel, stones, shale or slate, will dry quickly, even after heavy rain. Plants growing in it will be among the first to suffer in drought.

Such soils are generally low on plant foods, because the mineral particles, being dissolved in the soil water, go with it as it passes through. However, in spring the sun will warm it up before most other soil types and, because the particles are not held together by minute electrical charges, as clay particles are, it is easy to dig and work.

A good many flowering plants actually like growing in such starved, dry soils, particularly those which come from the Mediterranean region. Many bulbs do especially well in the good drainage, and grow profusely from seed.

Soil improvement

You can overcome both lack of food and lack of water by mixing in as much rotted organic matter as can be spared; 7 kg per sq m (15-16 lb per sq yd) is not too much. It is better to dig it in only a few weeks before planting or sowing, in late, rather than early, winter. Otherwise it breaks down so quickly that plants do not benefit from it. Mulches should be repeated during the growing season as they rot down, giving the last one in early fall.

But you may need to supplement the plant food by using fertilizers. For such soils the slow-acting organic ones are best, dried blood, hoof and hornmeal, or bonemeal. The first two contain mostly nitrogen, to be applied at up to 60 g per sq m (2 oz per sq yd), and the latter, phosphorus, up to 120-180 g per sq m (4-6 oz per sq yd). Wood-ash, for potassium, is good, at 120 g (4 oz), or sulphate of potash at 15-30 g (½-1 oz).

Mulching
On fast-draining soils it will be necessary to mulch repeatedly with leaf mould or other organic substances.

SELECTION OF PLANTS FOR WELL-DRAINED SOIL CONDITIONS (NOT CHALK)

PLANT	GROUP	COLOR/FLOWERING TIME	HEIGHT/SPREAD
Agapanthus	Herb. perennial (slightly tender)	Blue, white/ mid-late summer	90 × 75cms (36 × 30ins)
Broom	Shrub	All colors but blue/ spring-summer	prostrate-240 × 45-150cms (-96 × 18-60ins)
Escallonia	Shrub	Pink, red, white/ early midsummer	180 × 150cms (72 × 60ins)
Evening primrose	Herb. perennial	Yellow/ early summer-fall	30-60 × 30-60cms (12-24 × 12-24ins)
Geranium	Herb. perennial	Blue, purple, red, pink, white/summer	23-75 × 30-60cms (9-30 × 12-24ins)
Gladiolus	Corm	All colors/ early summer-mid fall	30-75 × 20cms (12-30 × 8ins)
Iris	Herb. perennial	All colors/ early summer	90 × 45cms (36 × 18ins)
Jerusalem sage	Shrub (slightly tender)	Yellow/ mid-summer	90 × 90cms (36 × 36ins)
Laburnum	Tree	Yellow/ late spring-early summer	450 × 360cms (180 × 144ins)
Lavender	Shrub	Mauve, blue, white/ midsummer	90 × 105cms (36 × 42ins)
Lupin	Herb. perennial	All colors early-midsummer	75-90 × 75cms (30-36 × 30ins)
Milfoil	Herb. perennial	Yellow/white midsummer	90 × 60cms (36-24ins)
Pinks/Carnations	Herb. perennial	Pink, red, white, salmon/ early-midsummer	1538 × 15-38cms (6-15 × 6-15ins)
Red hot poker	Herb. perennial	Orange, yellow/ mid-late summer	90-120 × 60-90cms (36-48 × 24-36ins)
Sea holly	Herb. perennial	Blue/ mid-late summer	90 × 60cms (36-24ins)
Senecio greyi	Shrub	Yellow/ midsummer	90 × 90cms (36 × 36ins)
Sun rose	Shrub	Yellow, red, orange/ summer	trailing-38 × 45cms (-15 × 18ins)
Tamarisk	Shrub, tree	Pink/ late spring, late summer	240-450 × 180-240cms (96-180 × 6-8ins)
Tulip	Bulb	All colors but blue/ spring-early summer	15-75 × 15-20cms (6-30 × 6-8ins)
Wintersweet	Shrub	Yellow/ early-mid winter	240 × 240cms (96 × 96ins)

Flowers for chalk soil

Although chalk soils are often thin, dry and lacking in any obvious nourishing substances, many plants seem to be quite happy with them. This is partly because the natural alkalinity of chalk offends very few plants, and partly because many plants appreciate the good drainage of chalk soils. The group of plants shown in this stylized border includes some – catmint, mallow (*Malva*), heathers and scabiosa – which have a distinct liking for chalk. Others, such as golden rod and coreopsis, will do well in any well-drained soil. The buddleia shown here is a deciduous type, but there are many buddleias and the group includes some evergreen kinds. Catnip, which used to be grown for its herbal properties, is a good border plant and has a long flowering season

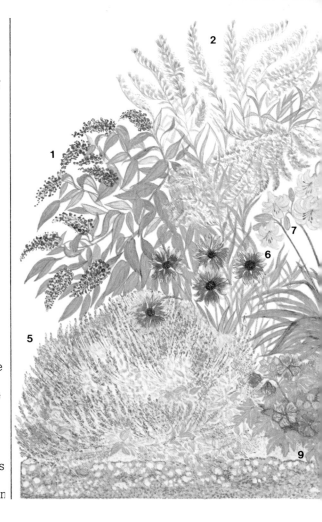

The chalk garden

1 Buddleia
deciduous shrub

2 Golden rod
herbaceous perennial

3 Coreopsis
herbaceous perennial

4 Clematis
deciduous climber

5 Catnip
herbaceous perennial

6 Gaillardia
herbaceous perennial

7 Day lily
herbaceous perennial

8 Scabiosa
herbaceous perennial

9 Musk mallow
herbaceous perennial

10 Heather
evergreen sub-shrub

Working with chalk (alkaline) soil

A chalky soil will have lumps of chalk in it, a grayish or whitish appearance, and may have pure chalk below the topsoil. Such soils will obviously have a very alkaline reaction, but fortunately there are few flowering plants which strongly object to this. The ones that do are noted in the tables – remember that there are also other acid-preferring plants besides those listed.

Reducing alkalinity

If you wish to reduce the alkalinity, you can do so slowly over a period of years by the regular addition of humus (rotted organic matter will supply this) and commercial fertilizers, which are often acid in reaction.

You can do it more quickly with *flowers of sulphur*, an average rate of application being 60 g per sq m (2 oz per sq yd), but this method is rather risky, as it produces all sorts of chemical reactions in the soil. The rate should vary according to the degree of alkalinity, and it is best to obtain expert advice before using it.

Soil improvement

The other problem with chalky soil is that it is usually quick-draining, and shallow into the bargain, so one way and another, it needs even more organic matter than sandy soil. Generous and frequent applications will go a long way to making it fit for plants to live in. These should be in the form of dressings dug-in late in winter or put on top in spring and summer.

As with any soil type of situation, there are plants which prefer chalk as part of their diet and environment. Some of these are given in the related table; you can also grow all those suggested for the well-drained soils except lupins.

PLANTS FOR LIME-FREE SOIL	
PLANT	GROUP
Celmisia	Alpine (perennial)
Erythronium	Hardy bulb
Fritillaria	Hardy bulb
Gaultheria	Evergreen shrub
Gentiana	Alpine (perennial)
Heather	Evergreen sub-shrub
Lily	Hardy bulbs
Meconopsis	Herbaceous perennial
Pieris	Evergreen shrub
Primula	Herbaceous perennial
Trillium	Hardy bulb

SELECTION OF PLANTS FOR ALKALINE SOIL CONDITIONS

PLANT	GROUP	COLOR/FLOWERING TIME	HEIGHT/SPREAD
Buddleia	Shrub	Purple, plum, red, white/ midsummer-early fall	210-270 × 270cms (84-108 × 84ins)
Californian Lilac	Shrub (slightly tender)	Blue/ midsmmer-mid fall	180-360 × 180-300cms (72-144 × 72-120ins)
Catnip	Herb. perennial	Blue/ early-midsummer, early fall	60 × 60cms (24 × 24ins)
Centaurea montana	Herb. perennial	Blue/ late spring-midsummer	45 × 45cms (18 × 18ins)
Clematis	Climber	Red, pink, mauve, blue, white/summer	300-450cms (120-180ins)
Coreopsis	Herb. perennial	Yellow/ summer	30-90 × 45cms (12-36 × 18ins)
Cotoneaster	Shrub	White/ early-midsummer	90-300 × 120-360cms (36-120 × 48-144ins)
Day lily	Herb. perennial	Orange, yellow, red/ mid-late summer	90 × 90cms (36 × 36ins)
Deutzia	Shrub	White, pink/ late spring-early summer	105-150 × 120cms (42-60 × 48ins)
Gaillardia	Herb. perennial	White, pink/ early summer-mid fall	60 × 60cms (24 × 24ins)
Golden rod	Herb. perennial	Yellow/ late summer-early fall	75-150 × 60-90cms (30-60 × 24-36ins)
Gypsophila	Herb. perennial	White, pink/ summer	23-90 × 60-90cms (9-36 × 24-36ins)
Heather	Shrub	Purple, pink, red, white/ late summer-early spring	15-23 × 20-35cms (6-9 × 10-15ins)
Leopard's Bane	Herb. perennial	Yellow/ early-mid spring	45-60 × 60cms (18-24 × 24ins)
Lilac	Shrub	Mauve, crimson, pink, white/late spring	450 × 360cms (180 × 144ins)
Mullein	Herb. perennial	Yellow, pink/ early summer-early fall	90-180 × 60-90cms (36-72 × 24-36ins)
Musk mallow	Herb. perennial	Pink, white/ summer	60-90 × 45-60cms (24-36 × 18-24ins)
Scabiosa	Herb. perennial	lavender, blue, white/ mid-late summer	60 × 60cms (24 × 24ins)
Solanum	Climber (slightly tender)	Purple/ summer-fall	450-600cms (180-240ins)
Syringa	Shrub	White/ early midsummer	180-300 × 180-300 (72-120 × 72-120ins)

Flowers for shade

It is not necessary to fill shady gardens, or the shady corners of a garden, with foliage plants. Although such places are ideal for many evergreens, the amount of color provided by rhododendrons and camellias is as varied and striking as any supplied by deciduous and herbaceous plants. Many of the spring flowering plants, especially lily of the valley and primulas, are native to woodland conditions and will thrive in parts of the garden which can present problems at other times of year. Some of the plants shown here are best with only light, or partial, shade – peony, periwinkle, lungwort *(Pulmonaria)* and London Pride *(Saxifraga)*. These plants require only to be protected from the most severe effects of sun.

The shady garden

1 Weigela *deciduous shrub*
2 Rhododendron *evergreen shrub*
3 Camellia *evergreen shrub*
4 Daffodil/Narcissus *bulbs*
5 Peony *herbaceous perennial*
6 Azalea *deciduous shrub*
7 Periwinkle *evergreen shrub*
8 Lily of the valley *herb. perennial*
9 Lungwort *herbaceous perennial*
10 London Pride *herb. perennial*
11 Polyanthus *herb. perennial*
12 Primula *herbaceous perennial*

COPING WITH SHADE

If the shade is caused by a small or moderately-sized tree, you may be able to improve the situation by pruning.

Cutting side shoots

Using pruning saw

Pruning & lopping
If trees in your garden are very overgrown the normal processes of pruning, and sometimes lopping, will produce some improvement in the light. Remove first any damaged and weak branches; cut out any shoots that are growing into the center, then remove crossing branches. Always remove branches in a way that retains the outline of the tree.

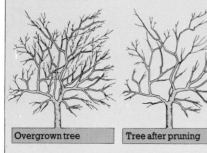

Overgrown tree | **Tree after pruning**

Shady situations

Most plants which flower need sun. But a shaded site does not necessarily mean that no flowering plants can be grown. There are degrees of shade: it may be dappled, for example, as in light woodland. It may be in shade for only part of the day, or partially in shade for the whole day.

If the site is in deep shade, it is not reasonable to expect anything to grow except ferns and mushrooms. But gardens are rarely made on such sites, so you should be able to grow some of the plants listed in the table.

Some of them actually do better, with a little shade, and some of the clematis hybrids, which like alkaline soils, are more deeply colored if they face north or are not exposed to the midday sun.

The soil in a shady place is not necessarily permanently wet. Close to walls and fences facing north, or under the umbrella of large trees, the soil is frequently dry, if not actually dusty.

If so, it is important to prepare it well by digging in extra garden compost or manure, and giving the plants a superthick mulch when the soil is moist, so that it stays damp.

SELECTION OF PLANTS FOR SHADY CONDITIONS

PLANT	GROUP	COLOR/FLOWERING TIME	HEIGHT/SPREAD
Anemone/Japanese	Herb. perennial	White, pink/ late summer-fall	120 × 90cms (48 × 36ins)
Camellia ★	Shrub	Pink, red, white/ spring	300 × 300cms (120 × 120ins)
Christmas Rose	Herb. perennial	White/ winter	30 × 45cms (12 × 18ins)
Columbine ○	Herb. perennial	All colors/ late spring-midsummer	45-75 × 30cms (18-30 × 12ins)
Daffodils/Narcissi ○	Bulb	Yellow, white, orange/ spring	15-60 × 10-15cms (6-24 × 4-6ins)
Heuchera	Herb. perennial	Pink, red, white/ late spring-midsummer	45 × 45cms (18 × 18ins)
Honeysuckle ○	Hardy climber	Cream, pink/ midsummer-mid fall	540 × 450cms (216 × 180ins)
Hydrangea ○	Shrub	Pink, blue, white/ midsummer-mid fall	90-150 × 90-150cms (36-60 × 36-60ins)
Jasmine/Winter	Hardy climber	Yellow/ late autumn-late winter	360 × 300cms (144 × 120)
Lily	Bulb	All colors but blue/ midsummer-early fall	23-240 × 15-23cms (9-96 × 6-9ins)
Lily-of-the-valley	Herb. perennial	White/ late spring	15cms × spreading (6ins × spreading)
London's Pride	Herb. perennial	Pink/ late spring-early summer	30cms × spreading (12ins × spreading)
Lungwort	Herb. perennial	Blue, pink, purple, red/ spring	30-45 × 30cms (12-18 × 12ins)
Peony ○	Herb. perennial	Pink, carmine, white/ late spring-early summer	45-90 × 60cms (18-36 × 24)
Periwinkle	Trailing perennial	Blue, white, purple/ spring-summer	30cms × spreading (12ins × spreading)
Primula spp (inc. primrose, polyanthus)	Herb. perennial	All colors/ spring-summer	10-90 × 10-30cms (4-36 × 4-12ins)
Rhododendron/ Azalea ★ ○	Shrub	All colors/ spring-summer	30-180+ × 45-180cms (12-72+ × 18-72ins)
Weigela	Shrub	Pink, red, white/ late spring-early summer	180-300 × 150-210cms (72-120 × 60-84ins)
Witch Hazel ★	Shrub	Yellow/ winter	210 × 150cms (84 × 60ins)

○ = Half Shade   ★ = Acid-neutral soil requirement

Flowers for sunny gardens

Most flowering plants like a certain amount of sun, but very few respond well to unrelenting heat. In temperate climates this is rarely a problem, but if you have a site which has little or no shade you should exercise some care in choosing plants. Of those shown here, sedum, rock rose (*Cistus*) and aubretia are particularly well-suited to exposed sites. Aubretia is more usually grown on walls and steps than in borders. Salvias are also good for sunny positions. This is a very big group of plants which includes the popular herb, sage. The example shown here is *S. sclarea*, better known as clary, a plant usually grown for its blue and pink bracts rather than its flowers. Two veronicas are shown here: the blue one is *V. teucrium* and the white is *V. virginica* 'Alba'.

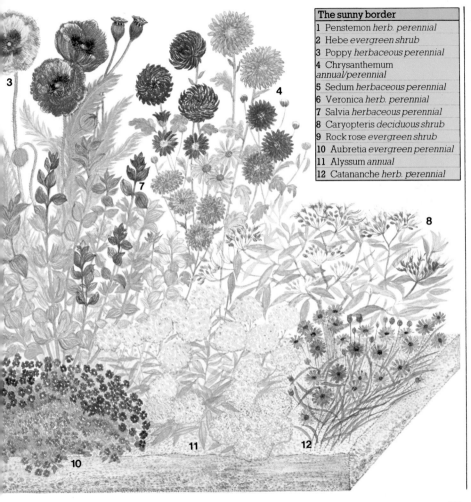

DEALING WITH SUNNY SITES

Too much sun may seem to be the ideal problem, but it can be disastrous.

Choose the right plants

Use a sprinkler

Give plants plenty of water

Take precautions
The best precaution you could take in this situation, would be to grow only those plants which will tolerate a considerable amount of heat and direct sunlight. The opposite page lists 20 of such plants. If you can provide some shade, either artificially or by planting trees, so much the better. If you cannot do this, make sure that you give the plants an adequate supply of water – and do not underestimate the amount that they will need. A sprinkler is the best watering device. If you must water by hose, you will have to spend lengthy periods spraying your plants.

Sunny situations

Blazing sun is all very well, but the only plants that really relish it are the cacti. Although gardeners in temperate climates mostly cry out for sun, prolonged hot sunshine can cause a lot of trouble.

If you have a sunny garden, you can grow the majority of flowering plants, provided you ensure that the soil contains enough moisture. The soil in such areas may be dry from the heat of the sun, or because it is light and quick-draining. If you cannot spare the time to water frequently and heavily, the selection of plants will be considerably restricted, and you will have to be careful in your choice.

Plants which do well in sun are those with gray-green or silvery-gray leaves. The dryness of the surface soil in winter ensures that the crown does not rot at soil level, and the covering of wax or hairs on the leaves enables them to withstand heat and sun better than the unprotected green-foliage plants.

You can, reduce the effects of sun by planting shrubs and trees, or by artificial barriers, and you may have to do this if the site is open to the east or north wind.

SELECTION OF PLANTS FOR SUNNY GARDENS

PLANT	GROUP	COLOR/FLOWERING TIME	HEIGHT/SPREAD
Alyssum	Herb. perennial	Yellow/ mid spring-early summer	15-25 × 45cms (6-10 × 18ins)
Aubrieta	Herb. perennial	Purple, red, pink, blue-mauve/spring	carpeting
Caryopteris x clandonensis	Shrub	Blue/ fall	90 × 120cms (36 × 48ins)
Catananche caerulea	Herb. perennial	Blue/ early summer-fall	60 × 60cms (24 × 24ins)
Chrysanthemum (inc. Korean)	Herb. perennial	All colors but blue/ late summer-late fall	23-120 × 30-75cms (9-48 × 12-30ins)
Hebe	Shrub	Mauve, red pink, white, blue/ early summer-mid fall	23-135 × 60-180cms (9-54 × 24-72ins)
Hibiscus	Shrub	Blue-purple, crimson, pink, white/ late summer-early fall	150 × 120cms (60 × 48ins)
Hyacinth	Bulb	All colors/ spring	23 × 12cms (9 × 5ins)
Mexican orange blossom	Shrub	White/ late spring-mid fall	150 × 180cms (60 × 72ins)
Ornamental onion	Bulb	Purple, pink, lilac, red, white/summer	15-120 × 15-30cms (6-48 × 6-12ins)
Passion flower	Climber (slightly tender)	Blue, purple and white/ midsummer-fall	300-450cms (120-180ins)
Penstemon	Herb. perennial	Purple, pink, red, white blue/summer fall	25-90 × 60cms (10-36 × 24ins)
Peruvian Lily	Perennial (slightly tender)	All colors but blue/ mid-late summer	90-120 × 30-60cms (36-48 × 12-24ins)
Plumbago	Shrub	Blue/ midsummer-mid fall	75 × 120cms (30 × 48ins)
Poppy	Herb. perennial	Red, pink, white/ late spring-early summer	90 × 90cms (36 × 36ins)
Rock rose	Shrub (slightly tender)	Pink, magenta, purple, white/summer	15-156 × 90-120cms (6-66 × 36-84ins)
Salvia	Herb. perennial	Blue, purple/ summer-fall	45-105 × 30-60cms (18-42 × 12-24ins)
Sedum spectabile	Herb. perennial	Pink, red, magenta/ late summer-mid fall	23-45 × 30-45cms (9-18 × 12-18ins)
Veronica	Herb. perennial	Blue, pink, white/ summer-fall	30-75 × 45-60cms (12-30 × 18-24ins)
Wallflower	Biennial	All colors but blue and mauve/ spring-early summer	30-60 × 23-30cms (12-24 × 9-12ins)

Color all year round

Filling the flowerless gaps

Most of the gardens which rely on flowers to provide color are certainly very colorful during the spring and for some of the summer and early fall. But there are often gaps in the sequence, especially in winter, a time when the majority of plants are dormant and the weather discourages work in the garden.

However, there are plenty of plants which will bloom during the gaps, and it is only a question of tracking them down from catalogue descriptions.

In spring the flowers of bulbs and many shrubs can provide a dazzling display throughout the season. In summer, the herbaceous perennials, the annuals and the bedding plants take over the center of the stage, and in fall, there is a tremendous final flare-up from the dahlias, chrysanthemums and Michaelmas daisies.

Throughout the year, plants from other groups will be in flower: bulbs in fall including nerines, autumn crocus and colchicum; primulas and wallflowers in spring, and in summer a succession of shrubs – hibiscus, hydrangeas, mock orange (philadelphus) and fuchsias, for example.

Filling the gaps

In temperate climates, it can be difficult to fill the gaps between seasons with color. The spring garden in May, *right*, full of wallflowers, forget-me-nots and tulips, will look barren a month later, and the summer show of annuals, *below*, will give way to some empty patches in fall – although the petunias will struggle on. The other small garden, *below right*, contains some long-flowering plants and a good variety of foliage to help through the lean periods. For fall color, dahlias, *top left*, are superb, for the difficult early spring, crocuses, *below left*, are unbeatable.

Planning all year color

When you are deciding what to grow, so that there are plants in flower somewhere in the garden at all times of the year, the time at which a particular plant flowers is its most important characteristic. This may seem transparently obvious, but is surprising how often it is forgotten or ignored.

Many gardeners tend to choose plants that they know and like, or plants whose catalogue or book illustration shows them to be particularly ornamental. This almost inevitably results in spasmodic masses of flower at intervals, instead of a nicely-timed flow of blooms right through the year.

Surprisingly, one of the periods when flowers are few and far between, is early summer. The spring rush of plants to get into flower as soon as the cold weather is over is followed by a pause while the summer flowers get into their stride, and it is worth looking for plants which start to bloom in late spring and for those which start early in midsummer, in the expectation that they will overlap.

Late fall is a very difficult time to obtain color, more so than winter. But there are some shrubs and trees, such as mahonia cultivars, fall-flowering cherry, winter jasmine and laurustinus, to name a few, and roses will often continue to bloom into early winter.

In mild fall, herbaceous plants will go on flowering long after their normal season, and there is a species of violet which starts to flower in mid fall and goes on through winter. Some spring-flowering shrubs will have a repeat performance: the Mexican Orange-blossom (*Choisya ternata*) is a good example.

Encouraging long flowering

With the protection of cloches, you can encourage bulbs and herbaceous perennials to flower earlier and go on longer. Careful pruning of shrubs plays its part, too, in ensuring that they flower their natural season. Some spring-flowering plants, e.g. aubrieta, will flower in autumn if they are cut back as soon as they have finished in spring.

A good way of discovering the gaps in the flower succession is to make a chart listing the plants, with the weeks of the year running across the top, and mark the time at which they are in flower. You can see then, at a glance, where flowers are non-existent or where they are rather sparse.

The natural garden

The natural garden is primarily an informal one, but this does not necessarily imply that it is a completely unrestricted jungle. There are two aims: one, to obtain a visually attractive garden and another, to supply an area in which birds, insects, reptiles, small mammals and soil organisms such as worms can live and breed safely.

You can, for instance, encourage butterflies, moths and pollinating insects such as bees by growing certain plants: buddleia, sedum, Michaelmas daisy, primrose, lavender, borage and scabiosa.

Attracting birds

Many birds are seed-eating, so flowers should be allowed to fruit. The single forms are best, as the doubles hardly ever set seed. Plants native to the country will encourage a variety of insects for the insect eaters; alder, bird cherry, holly, bramble, and what are generally called weeds are some that could be included.

Trees and shrubs are important to provide bird-nesting sites. Water in the garden is very desirable as a pool or stream, to supply homes for toads, frogs, etc., and to ensure that other fauna can always obtain water – bees frequently need to drink – and swallows need mud for nest-building.

Natural habitats

Paving, dry stone walls, stones and bricks round the pool or on a rock garden provide hiding-places for all sorts of creatures: chipmunks, hibernating ladybirds, and toads.

By planting a variety of types of plants, and by supplying a varied garden framework, to ensure protection and food, the wild life will be able to live and breed in it.

Organic matter mulches, ground-cover plants, and a complete refusal to use pesticides except in real emergencies, will maintain a tremendous mixture of living creatures in the garden. Careful choice of plants will produce a natural and beautiful garden, as well. Weeds often have, looked at dispassionately, ornamental and colorful flowers – rose-bay willow-herb and the field poppy are good examples. A natural garden that is not to be an unrestricted jungle will require a certain amount of control. Drastic cutting back, however, should be left until winter.

The site - basic considerations

Site characteristics

Whether you are dealing with a piece of land not yet cultivated or planted, have taken over an established garden, or are having a second look at the one you have been running for several years, there are several fundamental points to get clear.

Climatic conditions

What kind of climate and what kind of weather does your area have? Do you have a lot of frost and snow, cold springs and early falls? Or do you have mild winters when the temperature rarely drops below freezing, and the summers are regularly hot?

Is the annual rainfall heavy, do you have much cloud and fog, are there long hours of sunshine? Is there a great deal of light, as in flat country or coastal gardens?

If you can wait a year, it pays handsomely to discover the micro-climate of your garden - the parts of the garden that are shady and at what times of the year, the drafty places, the frost-pockets and the waterlogged patches. Where are the sheltered sun-traps? Which parts are open to the prevailing wind; what is the prevailing wind?

The aspect

Tied in with this is the aspect of the site: which way does it face: south, east, north or west? South or west facing will be a good deal warmer than north or east, especially if there is no barrier against the winds from these directions. But some plants like to face north, where it is cooler and less light.

Light and shade

The quality of light available is very important. A site overshadowed in part, if not altogether, by tall buildings or large trees will cut down considerably the choice of flowering plants which will grow there. Most plants need a good light, and sun for at least part of the day.

Dappled shade, similar to the light which filters through thin woodland, is much more acceptable. Heavier shade for part of the day is also permissible, especially if the sunny period occurs in the morning.

Soil type

Just as important as these considerations is the type of soil in the garden. Usually, one kind of soil predominates, but sometimes there are pockets of quite a different kind within it, different that is, with regard to structure, and acidity or alkalinity. You should, therefore, assess samples from several parts of the site.

The structure of a soil – the way in which crumbs are made up and hold together - influences the rate at which moisture passes through it. This, in turn, affects the retention of plant foods.

Soil consists of various ingredients: particles of clay, sand, chalk, grit, humus, organic matter, peat; also bacteria, fungi, insects and stones. Whichever type of particle predominates will determine the basic soil. Loam consists of a mixture of clay, sand, organic matter and silt in fairly equal proportions.

Planning

If you are dealing with an established but unknown flower garden, it is a good idea to make a plan and mark all the existing plants on it. Then decide what you would like to keep, and what is worth keeping, be ruthless with the remainder, and plant your own choice in the gaps. Be careful when first digging, in case there are dormant bulbs or perennials buried beneath the surface.

SOIL TESTING

The type of soil you have in your garden will greatly influence the choice of plants. Use the method described here to identify the soil type. Testing for alkalinity is not so important at this stage.

◀ **Soil texture**
The best way to establish the soil type is to crumble and squeeze a sample between your fingers. The characteristics of the main soil types are given below.

Clay soil
Grayish; very heavy when wet, tends to crack when dry.

Sandy soil
Feels gritty and will be very loose in dry conditions.

Shingly/Gravelly soil
Contains gravel or small stones. Not good as topsoil.

Chalk soil
May be shallow; usually contains flints and lumps of chalk.

Peat soil
Rich, dark brown; springy and flaky to the touch. Tends to be acid.

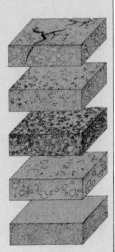

Tools and equipment

For flower gardening you will need the following basic collection of tools: digging fork, spade, hand fork or trowel, metal rake, watering-can with a fine and a coarse rose, a hoe, pruning shears, a knife, a strong pair of gloves and a wheelbarrow.

To this you can add later, a sprayer, bucket or basket, a measuring tape, step or pruning ladders, a pruning saw, loppers, an edging tool and a hose with a sprinkler attachment.

It is very well worth buying what may at first appear to be expensive tools. They last very much longer, a lifetime if you are careful, and they will stand up to very hard, tough work without twisting, breaking, or easily becoming blunt. In other words, buy the best that you can afford.

Look for tools which are made of forged steel with handles of a good hardwood. Make sure they are comfortable to hold, and are well balanced and of a comfortable weight for you.

Clean them after use, oil them if they are to be put away for the winter, and keep the cutting tools scrupulously sharp. Hacking away with a blunt blade ruins blade and plant.

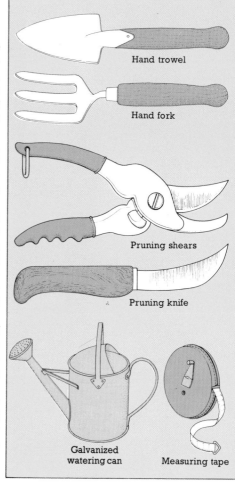

Hand trowel

Hand fork

Pruning shears

Pruning knife

Galvanized watering can

Measuring tape

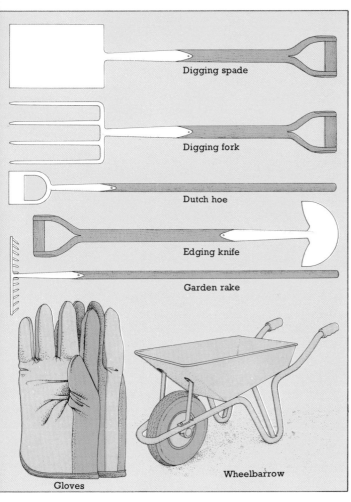

Digging spade

Digging fork

Dutch hoe

Edging knife

Garden rake

Gloves

Wheelbarrow

TOOLS

Hand tools
The trowel, fork and pruning tools shown here will be essential, but they should suffice for most close-range jobs.

Larger tools
Forks, spades, rakes and hoes are indispensible items of equipment and there are many types. But the selection shown here will do for most situations.

Other equipment
A wheelbarrow, gloves and watering can should complete your basic equipment.

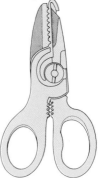

Flower shears
An exceptionally useful item for holding flowers as they are cut.

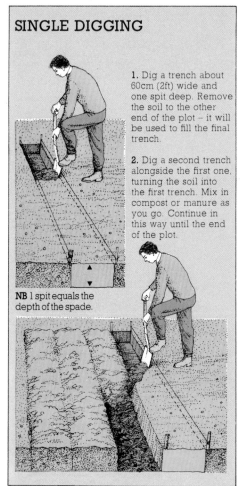

SINGLE DIGGING

1. Dig a trench about 60cm (2ft) wide and one spit deep. Remove the soil to the other end of the plot – it will be used to fill the final trench.

2. Dig a second trench alongside the first one, turning the soil into the first trench. Mix in compost or manure as you go. Continue in this way until the end of the plot.

NB 1 spit equals the depth of the spade.

Soil preparation

It is perfectly feasible to plant herbaceous perennials, shrubs or bulbs straight into the ground without digging or treating the soil in any way beforehand. But, unless you have exceptionally good soil, you will not get good results, and the plants are quite likely to have short lives and be unhealthy for much of them.

Digging

The longer a plant is going to live, the more thorough must be the soil preparation. Whereas you can get away with single digging, to one spade's depth, before planting annuals, bulbs and the smaller herbaceous perennials, the larger plants, shrubs and trees should have their planting sites double dug (to two spades' depth), and the bottom of the hole forked up as well.

Such digging should be done, at the very least, several weeks in advance to allow the soil to settle and absorb any materials which you have mixed into it. Rotted organic matter such as farm manure, leafmould or garden compost will be necessary, in quantities suggested for the different types of soil. Slowly released nutrients such as bonemeal may also be required.

Clearing the ground

You can also take the opportunity to clear the ground thoroughly of weeds; it is essential to eliminate completely the perennial weeds, such as horsetail, bindweed and ground-elder, especially for shrub plantings or herbaceous borders. If any particles of root are missed, the weed will become inextricably entwined with the cultivated plant, and you will have constant trouble in controlling it.

When you dig the soil, remove all rubbish and large stones as well as weeds, and break up the large clods, so that it is of an even consistency and firmness, and reasonably level. A crumbly soil is the easiest one for roots to settle into and start to grow again.

If you are not intending to do any major planting or sowing until spring, it is a good idea to dig the soil in fall or early winter. This allows it to be well broken up by frost, exposes soil pests to predators and the cold, and ensures that additions are thoroughly absorbed.

For fall plantings, digging can be done early enough to allow the ground to fallow through the summer, so that all weed seeds germinate, and can be dealt with as they appear.

DOUBLE DIGGING

1 Dig a trench one spit deep and 90cm (3ft) wide. Remove the soil to the other end of the plot.
2 Dividing the trench in half lengthways, dig the first half another spit deep. Fork and manure the bottom of the deeper half.

3 Return the second spit soil to its own depth.
4 Dig a new trench, one spit deep and 45cm (18in) wide. Using the soil to fill the first half trench to surface level. Repeat these steps across the plot, making sure that second spit soil is always used to fill a second spit trench. Use the soil from the first trench to fill the last.

1 Digging first trench

2 Digging second spit

3 Returning soil

4 Digging new trench

USEFUL TIPS FOR SOWING

Preparing the ground
Before sowing, fork over the top few cms (ins) and rake the soil to a fine crumbly consistency. If there are many stones in the soil, you may need to sift the top few cms (ins).

Fork the top few cms (ins)

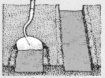

Making a flat bottomed drill

Drills for seed sowing can be made with a draw hoe or the edge of a rake. Drills will usually be trench shaped, *above*, or V-shaped. When drawing the soil back over the drill, make sure that you do not disturb the seeds.

Carefully rake soil over the seeds

Sowing and planting

As we shall see in the plant classification section (p.44) the groups of plants usually grown from seed are annuals, biennials, and half-hardy annuals. Others which are sometimes seed-raised are the trees and shrubs, and herbaceous perennials including bulbs.

Seed germination

Except for the half-hardy annuals, seed is sown outdoors, and the soil must be carefully prepared to ensure good germination. If seeds are to germinate at all, they must have moisture. Most must have a higher temperature of soil and air than they need in adult life, many require darkness, and there must be a food supply available, particularly of the mineral nutrient phosphorus.

Cold and too much moisture are likely to kill the seed or newly germinated seedling; soil pests and fungus diseases can also destroy them. A lumpy soil, full of large stones, weeds and general debris will slow down or halt germination as well.

Hence soil preparation is aimed at producing a fine, friable surface soil, which will enable water to trickle through it at an even, moderate rate. This can be achieved by forking the top few cm (in) after the initial digging, and then raking the surface until it is of a crumb-like consistency.

You should choose a day when the soil is moist but not sodden; if the soil sticks to your shoes or boots, then it is too wet. Rake off at the same time all the rubbish, tread the surface to make it evenly firm, and then rake finally. Sow the seed thinly, in rows or patches, and cover with fine soil, then put scarecrows in place.

A week before you expect to sow, dress the soil lightly with a phosphatic fertilizer such as superphosphate.

The herbaceous perennials and woody plants are generally sown in a nursery bed, thinned and left for a year or so before transplanting and final planting.

Planting
When planting, soil preparation is not quite so important, especially with the larger plants. Provided it has had the initial prepartion, is in good structural condition and has plenty of plant food, it need only have any weeds that may have invaded the site removed, just before planting.

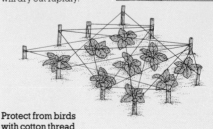

Frames and cloches

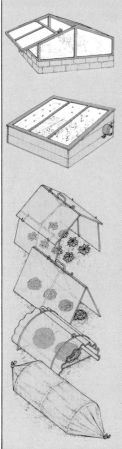

Frames
Frames can be heated or unheated, but for most gardeners, an unheated frame will suffice. Plants can be sown directly into frames or put in after potting on. The span roof type may have hinged or sliding panels and is usually unheated. The wooden framed type is based on the English light and can be fitted out with side wall heating.

Barn cloche
A traditional and effective glass type. Can be risky with children around. Easy to move around.

Tent cloche
Similar to the barn type and may be either glass or plastic.

Tunnel cloche
These are made from rigid plastic and are portable and cheap. They may discolor however.

Polyethylene tunnel
The cheapest type of cloche, but the polyethylene deteriorates rapidly.

Using frames and cloches

Most of the plants grown in flower gardening are hardy but, even so, by using protection such as frames and cloches, you can engineer a variety of cultural improvements.

Seed can be sown in frames, directly into the soil or into containers. The resulting plants will flower earlier and probably be stronger than those sown outdoors; fall-sown annuals, in particular, can benefit by being protected through the winter, especially sweet peas.

Frames can be used for plunging pots of alpines and bulbs resting through the summer or dormant in winter. They are also very useful for rooting all sorts of cuttings – soft and semiripe in containers, conifers and heathers directly into sand, and hardwood cuttings also directly, but into compost or good soil. Slightly tender perennial plants can be overwintered in them.

Cloches are useful for warming the soil of seed-beds before sowing in spring, and for protecting small plants with hairy or gray leaves from winter wet, which rapidly rots them. They can protect newly planted half-hardy annuals from cold.

Plant health

The garden plants which produce edible crops, such as fruit and vegetables, can be attacked and infected by a tremendous variety of plagues and pests, which seem to like eating them as much as we do.

The ornamental plants, on the other hand, are comparatively free at present of such troubles. Certainly, aphids and caterpillars are generally in evidence. There may be specific epidemics from year to year of, for instance, cockchafer, beetle, sawfly caterpillar, earwigs or leather-jackets (cranefly or daddy-long legs caterpillars).

Mildew and gray mould (*Botrytis cinerea*) are fairly widespread, the former near the end of a dry, hot summer in particular, the latter all through cool, damp weather. Roses are prone to black spot infection, except in town gardens.

But in general you will not have to be constantly at your flowering plants with sprayers, fungicides, insecticides, and surgical operations. Armed with bioresmethrin and sevin, malathion for really persistent pests, and benomyl, captan and sulphur dust for the fungus diseases, you should be able to deal with most above-ground infestations. Diazinon will cope with underground pests.

If you give your plants a good start at sowing or planting, provide suitably good soil, and supply food and water when either are needed and not naturally available, the plants will shrug off aliens without much difficulty.

The weather is probably the biggest enemy, in the form of extremes of rain, sun, wind, frost, hail, snow and lightning. Plant parts injured by any of these should be removed, or pared away to undamaged tissue.

CHEMICAL CONTROL

The chemicals listed below are some of the most effective and popular insecticides and fungicides.

CHEMICAL	USE
Bordeaux mixture	Fungal diseases
Benomyl	Soil-borne diseases
Diazinon*	Cabbage root-fly
	Aphids and other pests
Dinocap	Powdery mildew
Malathion*	Aphids and other pests
Thiram	Black spot, gray mould, rust
Zineb	Blight, mildew, rusts, mould
*These chemicals are poisonous to warm-blooded animals, including humans.	

Plant classification

Plant groups

In gardening books and articles you will often see plants referred to as 'herbaceous perennials', 'hardy annuals', 'shrubs', 'biennials' and so on. These words and phrases are a sort of shorthand for gardeners, which overcomes the necessity of having to use about five or ten words to describe a type of plant.

Basically plants, whether they are flowering or not, can be divided into two groups, one containing the plants with soft tissue, the other with hard or woody tissue. The flowering plants with soft tissue include all those in the groups: hardy annuals, half-hardy annuals, biennials, herbaceous perennials, and the bulbs, which are often taken to include corms and tubers.

Annuals

The annuals are plants grown from seed, which complete their life cycle within 12 months, often much more quickly. By 'life cycle' we mean the time they take to germinate, develop leaves and shoots, produce flowers and then set fruit containing the seed to provide the plants for the next generation.

Hardy annuals

The hardy annuals are usually sown outdoors in early or mid spring, and flower from midsummer until early fall. They will also survive the winter after a fall sowing with protection if the winter is severe, to start flowering in early summer or even late spring.

Half hardy annuals

The half-hardy annuals need much higher temperatures for germination in spring, so are sown in a heated propagator or greenhouse. They are then kept warm until the outdoor temperature has risen sufficiently for them to be planted in the garden, usually in early summer. They can be sown in spring, or in late winter, but the earlier they are sown the earlier they will be ready for planting out, so the garden should be sheltered and mild. Half-hardy plants must be properly introduced to outdoor temperatures before planting.

This category also includes what are called bedding plants – plants put close together to provide a brilliant and massed display of color. Such planting arrangements are often seen in public parks and gardens.

Biennials

The biennials are also grown from seed and are practically all hardy, but they take two growing seasons to complete their life-cycle. They are generally sown in late spring or early summer, and produce leaves and shoots until the fall, when they become dormant until spring. From mid spring/early summer, they flower, set seed, and die.

These groups are nearly always started from seed, though cuttings are taken from some of the half-hardy annuals, rooted and kept in artificial warmth until the spring.

Herbaceous perennials

Herbaceous perennials are grown from seed, or by vegetative propagation, that is, by division or stem or root cuttings. Such plants may live for many years, dying down in fall to become dormant for the winter. Some, however, are evergreen, and do not lose their leaves altogether in winter.

Bulbs

Bulbs are also perennial and follow the same life-cycle. In botanical terms, they consist of the swollen bases of leaves, whereas *corms* are made up of a thick-ened and shortened stem. *Tubers* are the swollen part of a root, or a stem, usually underground. All these forms have been developed to store food while the plant rests.

Woody plants

The plants with woody tissue include the shrubs, roses, trees and the hardy climbing plants. There are climbing plants with soft tissue, but most of these are half-hardy.

All the hard-tissued plants have bark on the stems and trunks; they are mostly long-lived and are generally grown from various sorts of stem cuttings or by layering. Shrubs consist of a collection of stems coming from the roots at soil level, but trees have a single stem, or trunk, which starts to branch some distance above the ground. Some shrubs may only have one stem, but it begins to branch very close to soil level, and they still develop into a bushy type of plant.

Climbers consist of one or more long straggling stems, climbing up other plants by a variety of methods.

The hard-wooded plants can be grown from seed, but take years to flower and fruit.

Growing herbaceous plants

Most herbaceous plants are hardy perennials, which live from year, have fibrous roots and will flower at some time during the year. Some die down completely in fall, others keep their leaves throughout the winter.

They are easy to grow, and do not need much care once planted. The main jobs are to keep them clear of weeds, mulch them in spring or fall, stake those that need it, and feed with a compound fertilizer in early spring.

On the following pages, you will find instructions and tips for growing a number of the most popular herbaceous perennials. These are the plants which can be left in the ground where they were sown or planted for many years. They are likely to be the mainstays of most garden plans.

In middle to late fall, the plants can be tidied by cutting the flowered stems down to soil-level, and forking the soil round them, but if the garden is a cold one such growth can be left on the plant to protect the crown until spring.

Flower quality becomes less good each year in many plants, so they should be dug up, usually every 3 or 4 years, in mid fall, divided and the outside pieces of each plant replanted. The central part will be the oldest and should therefore be chopped up for compost.

Soil preparation and the method of planting are important. Soil should be dug at least a month in advance and, if possible, in the fall or spring 6 months ahead. Depth should be 2 spades for most plants, but sometimes the topsoil is shallow and only 1 spade's depth is possible.

Rotted manure, garden compost, leaf-mould or other decayed organic matter can be mixed in at the same time, about 4½ kg (10lb) per sq m (per sq yd) for average soil, 7 kg (15lb) or more for light soil and 2.5 kg (5lb) for heavy soil; the last-named should have coarse grit added as well at about 3.5 kg (7lb).

When planting, first cut back excessively long roots, and those which are torn or otherwise damaged. Dig a hole sufficiently wide to take the roots at their full spread, and make a shallow mound in the center. Sit the plant on this, space the roots out round and over this mound, and fill in with crumbly soil.

Firm down carefully with the heel, add more soil if necessary, rake or mulch, and water if rain is not expected.

The herbaceous perennials dealt with on the following pages are of the hardy kind. This means that they can live out-of-doors, without protection in most areas. Although they are not greatly demanding of time and effort, they do require a reasonable amount of space. The small town garden is not, perhaps, ideal for them. The traditional herbaceous border needs the backing of a wall or hedge, a length of at least 6m (20ft) and plenty of space in front.

CULTIVATION TIPS

In general, herbaceous perennials require very little maintenance, but there are a few jobs to be done regularly – apart from weeding and watering.

Flower stems without leaves

Flower stems with leaves

Removing dead flowers
The heads of all faded flowers should be removed. This concentrates the resources of the plant into the formation of new flowers rather than seeds. Plants with single flower stems that are devoid of foliage should be cut back to ground level.

Plants which have leaves growing on the flower stems should be cut back to just below the top leaves.

Mulching
The spreading of organic matter, such as garden compost or leafmould, around the base of plants helps to conserve moisture and provides extra nutrition.

Agapanthus
Herbaceous perennial

Groups	the hardiest kinds are the Headbourne hybrids, height and spread: 60-90 × 60-75 cm (24-36 × 24-30 in), shades of blue, mid-late summer; *A. orientalis,* 45-60 × 60 cm (18-24 × 24 in), blue or white, summer; evergreen
Site/soil	sun and shelter, heavy, moist, deep soil
Soil preparation	dig 2 spades deep and mix in rotted organic matter, and slow-acting organic fertilizer in late winter
Sow/plant	plant in mid spring, and spread the fleshy roots out well, taking care to avoid injury; water in if the soil is dry
Cultivate	keep well watered in dry weather; liquid-feed from early summer until the flowers open; mulch in late spring annually, and protect crowns through winter; leave undisturbed until flower quality begins to deteriorate
Increase	by division in spring; plants grown from seed may not flower for two years
Troubles	severe cold will injure or kill them; they can be grown successfully in large pots which can be stood out during the summer and brought into a cool greenhouse in the fall; Headbourne hybirds, however, can be kept permanently out of doors if the situation is sheltered and sunny

Agapanthus
The agapanthus, or African lily, was first identified in South Africa during the 17th Century.

Pot grown plants
Agapanthus require large pots, so put in plenty of drainage material.

Border carnation
Herbaceous perennial

Groups	*Dianthus caryophyllus* (Clove Pink, Carnation), height and spread: 30-60 × 45 cm (12-24 × 18 in), red, mid–late summer, strongly fragrant; named hybrids derived from this species; they are further divided into *cloves, selfs* (one color), *fancies* with 2 or more colors splashed or flaked on to the basic color, and *picotees* with a pencil edging to the petals of a different color to the base color
Site/soil	sunny, well-drained, slightly limy soil
Soil preparation	dig 1 spade deep and mix a little rotted manure or garden compost with it in early fall or early spring
Sow/plant	plant in mid autumn or mid spring; plant firmly, in firm soil
Cultivate	keep clear of fallen leaves in winter; supply 45 cm (18 in) stakes in spring; feed with bonemeal in mid spring at 120 g per sq m (4 oz per sq yd); keep weeded, and mulch annually in spring; disbud in early summer to leave top bud and 4 others, spaced out; place tie round lower part of flower to prevent petals bursting out of green sheath; remove finished flowers
Increase	by layering after flowering, plant rooted layers 4-6 weeks later
Troubles	red spider mite; slugs in winter

Carnation
The genus *Dianthus* is very old, but border carnations have been extensively developed and there are a great many varieties.

Cut flowers
Carnations should be cut before the flowers are fully open, then stood up to their necks in water for 12 hours.

Border pink
Herbaceous perennial

Groups	Pinks are *Dianthus plumarius* (Cottage pink), height and spread: 30 × 30 cm (12 × 12 in), red, pink or white, late spring-late summer; named hybrids derived from the foregoing can be pink, white, red, maroon, chocolate and crimson, 23 × 60 cm (9 × 24 in), summer; 'Dad's Favorite', white with chocolate markings, and 'Mrs Sinkins', fragrant double white, are two good ones
Site/soil	sunny, well-drained, slightly limy soil
Soil preparation	dig 1 spade deep in early spring or early fall and mix in a little rotted farm manure or garden compost (not leafmould or peat); add grit if necessary
Sow/plant	plant in mid fall or early spring 23-30 cm (9-12 in) apart
Cultivate	liquid-feed in late spring and early summer; reduce flower-buds to 4 if larger blooms are required; remove blooms as soon as they have faded
Increase	by stem cuttings taken in late summer, and put into a shaded outdoor frame; then planted in early-mid fall by division in spring; they may also be raised from seed sown in a greenhouse during spring
Troubles	red spider mite in hot dry summers; caterpillars making webs on the leaves and buds

Cottage pink
single

Pinks can be single, semi-double or double. Most of the popular garden varieties are double.

Cutting pinks
Cut when the flowers are not quite open, using small, sharp scissors.

Christmas and Lenten rose

Herbaceous perennial

Groups	Christmas rose *(Helleborus niger)*, height and spread: 15-35 × 20-30 cm (6-15 × 8-12 in), white, mid-late winter; Lenten Rose *(H. orientalis)* and hybrids, 60 × 45 cm (24 × 18 in), cream, pink, purple, late winter-mid spring; Christmas and Lenten roses together will have a flowering season which lasts from mid winter to early spring
Site/soil	a little shade, deep fertile soil
Soil preparation	dig 2 spades deep and mix plenty of rotted organic matter with the soil, also grit if heavy
Sow/plant	plant early-mid fall 30 cm (12 in) apart and water in if the soil is dry
Cultivate	place cloche over Christmas Rose in early winter, to protect flowers from mud and encourage early blooming; mulch in mid spring annually, and keep well-watered in dry weather; liquid-feed occasionally in summer; leave undisturbed for as long as possible
Increase	by division in mid fall, use small rather than large pieces; do not lift and divide until they are becoming overcrowded; seeds can be slow to germinate
Troubles	slugs attack new shoots, bait essential; fungus diseases sometimes affect plants in spring, spray with a copper fungicide

Christmas rose
Hellebores are often regarded as plants for the specialist, but *Helleborus niger* and *H. orientalis* are suitable for most gardeners.

Cutting back
Both Christmas and Lenten roses benefit from being cut back to ground level immediately after flowering.

Chrysanthemum
Herbaceous perennial

Groups	Korean chrysanthemums, *C. sipiricum* cultivars, height and spread: 23-90 × 30-60 cm (9-36 × 12-24 in), single, double and pompom, all colors but blue, early-late fall; *C. rubellum* cultivars, 60-90 × 75 cm (24-36 × 30 in), single or semi-double, pink, red, bronze, yellow, white, purple, late summer-mid fall
Site/soil	sun, well-drained medium loam
Soil preparation	dig 1 spade deep in late fall or winter, and mix in rotted organic matter
Sow/plant	plant in early/mid spring, and supply stakes
Cultivation	keep well-watered in dry weather, and mulch every year in late spring; protect crowns in severe winter weather; dig up and replant every 3rd year. Pinching out the growing tips in late spring, and restricting the resulting branches to 5 or 6, will encourage bigger blooms and bring forward the flowering season
Increase	by division in spring
Troubles	mildew, leafminer, earwigs; spray benomyl or captan, for the first and dimethoate for the last two; pick off leaves infested with leafminer if not too many; try upturned pots containing newspaper or straw for the earwigs

Chrysanthemum
single

Chrysanthemums were introduced to the West from Japan in the 18th Century, but they had been grown in Japan for over 1000 years.

Protect blooms
Wrapping the blooms in greaseproof bags will protect them from severe weather.

Cut flowers
Flowers will last longer if you 'bruise' the end of the stem.

Cranesbill
Geranium, herbaceous perennial

Groups	the species of *Geranium* and their cultivars and hybrids of which there are many, flowering in summer in shades of pink, purple, lilac, blue, crimson and white; heights vary from 10-100 × 30-75 cm (6-42 x 12-30 in). 'Ballerina' (lilac), 'Johnson's Blue', *renardii* (white), *sanguineum* 'Splendens' (pink), and 'Buxton's Variety' (blue), are particularly good. These are true geraniums; bedding 'geraniums', which are really pelargoniums, should be regarded as greenhouse plants
Site/soil	sun, well-drained light, fertile soil
Soil preparation	dig 1 spade deep and add rotted organic matter, also grit if the soil is heavy, in early fall or winter; fork a dressing of a commercial compound fertilizer into the top few cm (in) a week before planting, if the soil is light
Sow/plant	plant mid fall or spring, in groups of 3/4
Cultivate	liquid-feed occasionally during summer if growing in light soil; dig up and replant if flowering begins to deteriorate
Increase	by division mid fall or early-mid spring
Troubles	occasionally caterpillars eating leaves, and some danger from slugs

Geranium
Cranesbills can provide color from mid-spring to early fall some species flowering throughout the summer.

Pot sowing
Sow seeds in pots and put into a cold frame until the seedlings have two pairs of leaves.

Delphinium
Herbaceous perennial

Groups	garden hybrids bred from *D. elatum*, height and spread: 210 × 90cm (84 × 36in); Belladonna hybrids from *D. belladonna*, 90 × 60cm (36 × 24in), with looser spikes and a branching habit; both kinds shades of blue, mauve, white and cream; *D. nudicaule* and hybrids, 90 × 60cm (36 × 24in), shades of red and pink; all flower early–midsummer
Site/soil	sun, shelter from wind, deep rich soil
Soil preparation	dig at least 2 spades deep, if the topsoil is deep enough, in winter or early spring, and mix in rotted organic matter, also bonemeal, 180 g per sq m (6 oz per sq yd)
Sow/plant	plant in mid spring very firmly, in groups of three, and stake in tripod formation
Cultivate	tie flowering stems to stakes as they grow; keep well watered in dry weather; liquid-feed from midsummer until fall and mulch in early spring; dig up and replant every 3-4 years, in early spring
Increase	from seed sown outdoors in late spring, transplanting to permanent positions in early fall; from cuttings of new shoots taken in early spring and put into pots in a cold frame; rooting takes 6-8 weeks
Troubles	slugs eat young shoots; caterpillars and mildew may attack leaves

Delphinium
Belladonna hybrid
Delphiniums are impressive plants and may easily grow to 2m (6.5 ft). Belladonna hybrids are smaller.

Staking plants
Support Delphiniums with stakes encircled with garden twine.

Lupin
Herbaceous perennial and shrub

Groups	*Lupinus polyphyllus* and varieties in blue, white and pink, height and spread: 90 × 60cm (36 × 24in); Russell hybrids, all colors 75-90 × 75cm (30-36 × 30in), less strong than the first group; *L. arboreus* (tree lupin), short-lived, fast-growing shrub, blue, yellow, white; all flower early summer
Site/soil	sun or a little shade, sandy, acid soil
Soil preparation	dig 2 spades deep late winter or early autumn, mix in rotted organic matter
Sow/plant	plant in late fall or early spring; use a trowel and spread fleshy roots out well, so that they are not broken in too small a hole; supply 4 stakes to each plant
Cultivate	thin out weak shoots to leave about 5 strong ones; remove flowerheads immediately flowering has finished; this will encourage 2nd crop of blooms in late summer; mulch in mid fall, also late spring if soil very light; feed in early spring with slow-acting fertilizer; dig up every 4 years or so, and renew
Increase	by root cuttings put in a temperature of 10°C (50°F) in late winter; by stem cuttings of young shoots, as delphiniums; by seed, sown outdoors mid spring and planted in position in summer; lupins are among the most easily grown of border plants

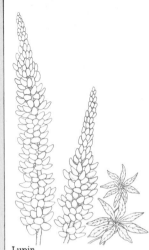

Lupin
flower and foliage
Lupins, now among the most popular of garden flowers, have been developed from a plant native to California.

Troubles
Yellowing of leaves (chlorosis); wilting in alkaline soil; slugs on young shoots – put slug pellets around seedlings.

Michaelmas daisy

Herbaceous perennial

Groups	*Aster novii-belgii* cultivars, height and spread: 75-120 × 60-90cm (30-48 × 24-36in), purple, magenta, blue, pink, white, crimson, early-mid fall; dwarf hybrids, bushy to 45 × 30cm (18 × 12 in) similar colors and flowering time; *Aster amellus* cultivars, 60 × 60cm (24 × 24 in), large flowers, late summer – mid fall
Site/soil	sun, deep moist, heavy soil; *A. amellus* kinds like lime in the soil
Soil preparation	dig 2 spades deep and mix in plenty of rotted organic matter in late summer or winter, depending on planting time
Sow/plant	plant early fall preferably, or in early – mid spring
Cultivate	stake tall-growing kinds when about 30cm (12in) tall, removing all but the best 5 shoots or so; place the stakes at an angle pointing away from the plant, and tie the shoots singly to them; also thin the *A. amellus,* kinds, but not so severely, and stake; keep well-watered in dry weather; dig up and replant every 3 years
Increase	by division in spring
Troubles	mildew in late summer; eelworm on dwarf cultivars in particular; wilt; spray benomyl or dinocap for first; dig up and burn plants infected with last two

Michaelmas daisy
These plants are among the most reliable of late flowering types, producing abundant blooms until the arrival of frost.

Cut back
All stems should be cut back to ground level immediately after flowering.

Peony
Herbaceous perennial

Groups	Common peony *(P. officinalis)* and hybrids, height and spread: 60-75 × 60cm (24-36 × 24in), red, white, pink, single and double, late spring; Chinese peony *(P. lactiflora)*, 75-105 × 60cm (30-42 × 24in), and hybrids, pink, white, red, crimson, single and double, some fragrant, early summer (N.B., there are also tree peonies, not very ornamental, except for *P. suffruticosa,* a beautiful plant but difficult to grow)
Site/soil	sun or half-shade, deep, well-broken down, heavy soil
Soil preparation	dig at least 2 spades deep, and mix in rotted organic matter, and bonemeal at 120g per sq m (4oz per sq yd)
Sow/plant	plant mid-late fall, make sure the holes are sufficiently large for the roots, and put the crowns 1-2.5cm (1-2in) deep, any deeper will delay or prevent flowering; space 90cm (36in) apart and water in if the soil is on the dry side
Cultivate	mulch generously in fall or late winter and keep well watered in dry weather; liquid-feed regularly from the time the flower buds appear, to flowering; leave undisturbed for many years
Increase	by division in mid fall – take care not to damage the brittle rootstock

Peony
The common peony was grown in Italy and southern France in the mid 16th Century. It may have been brought from Greece much earlier.

Troubles
Buds may wilt without opening: give them extra potash and make sure that the soil is in good condition. Young shoots sometimes wilt in spring, remove them and apply Bordeaux powder to the plant.

Dividing rootstock
Using a sharp knife, cut the rootstock into pieces making sure that each piece has several tubers. Remove any parts that are dead or rotting. Plant with the crowns just below soil level.

Phlox
Herbaceous perennials

Groups	*Phlox paniculata* cultivars, height and spread: 60-90 × 60cm (24-36 × 24in), pink, purple, blue, red, white, salmon, midsummer–early fall; *P. douglasii* and *P. subulata* cultivars, prostrate and mat-forming, mauve, pink, blue, red-purple, white; late spring–midsummer
Site/soil	sun and well-drained, rich soil for dwarf kinds; sun or a little shade, and deep, moderately heavy soil for tall kinds
Soil preparation	dig 1 spade deep in winter, mix in grit if soil is not sandy, and add leafmould or peat; tall kinds, dig 2 spades deep in early fall or winter, and mix in rotted organic matter
Sow/plant	plant dwarf kinds 23cm (9in) apart as edgings in early–mid-spring; tall ones mid autumn or early spring, in clumps
Cultivate	keep dwarf kinds free of weeds until well-established and spreading, dig up in early spring only when they have outgrown their space; liquid feed tall kinds in summer and fall, and mulch in early spring annually; keep well supplied with water in dry weather; remove weakest shoots before flowering
Increase	dwarf kinds by division in early spring; tall kinds by root cuttings in late summer, put vertically into pots or boxes of compost

Phlox
There are about 60 species of phlox, some of which are annuals. Many of the border phloxes are strongly scented.

Troubles
Stem and leaf eelworm. Burn infected plants and increase from unaffected root cuttings in new soil.

Poppy
Herbaceous perennial and annual

Groups	**perennial,** *Papaver orientale* and hybrids, height and spread: 90 × 60cm (36 × 24in), red, pink, white, early summer; Iceland poppy *(P. nudicaule)*, 30cm (12in), orange, pink, yellow, white, late spring–early fall; **annual,** Shirley Poppy, *(P. rhoeas)*, 30-60cm (12-24in), all colors but blue, single and double, summer; California Poppy *(Eschscholzia californica)*, 30-60 cm (12-24 in), shades of orange in spring
Site/soil	sun and well-drained soil; deep and fertile for perennials
Soil preparation	dig 2 spades deep and mix in rotted organic matter for perennials in winter; dig 1 spade deep in spring for annuals, and add organic matter if very sandy
Sow/plant	plant perennials spring; sow annuals outdoors where they are to grow in mid spring, barely cover with fine soil; Iceland poppies can be short-lived perennials but are usually treated as biennials or annuals
Cultivate	mulch perennials generously in mid spring annually; thin annuals to 7cm (3in), keep clear of weeds
Increase	perennials from root cuttings in mid winter, or by division in early spring; annuals from seed
Troubles	occasionally slugs on new shoots

Oriental poppy

The poppy which is now so widespread in gardens, was found near the Caspian sea.

Using poppy seeds
Poppy seeds for decorating cakes and breads can be obtained by cutting off the seed pods with about 20cm (8in) of stem and hanging them in a warm place until they are dry.

59

Primula
Herbaceous perennial

Groups	**primroses,** height and spread: 10×15cm (4×6in), yellow, white, spring; **polyanthus,** several flowers clustered on one stem, 15×15cm (6×6in), yellow, orange-red, pink, white, crimson, blue, spring; **primula** species such as *P.florindae,* 60-90cm (24-36in) yellow, *rosea,* pink, 15cm (6in) and *denticulata,* pale purple, 30cm (12in), all mid–late spring
Site/soil	dappled shade, moist, well-drained soil
Soil preparation	dig 1 spade deep, mix in leafmould or peat, and grit if soil is heavy
Sow/plant	sow seed in late summer in 7.5cm (3in) deep boxes in cold frame, using seed compost; mix seed with fine sand to ensure even sowing and just cover with fine compost; prick out seedlings when large enough to handle the following spring and transplant to flowering positions in early fall, 15cm (6in) apart
Cultivate	keep well supplied with water at all times, especially seed compost; mulch with rotted organic matter after transplanting; dig up after flowering
Increase	by offsets from old flowered plants, plant 15cm (6in) apart in a shady place until fall, then plant in flowering beds; by seed as above

Primula denticulata
The species shown above was discovered in the Himalayas in the 1840s.

Troubles
Slugs and snails; leaf-spots, spray with zineb; aphids, use bioresmethrin.

Sowing
When sowing, mix the seed with fine sand to give a more even distribution.

Annuals

The annual flowering plants are a group which complete their life cycle within a year, that is, they germinate, flower, set seed and die in 12 months. They are easily grown and brilliantly colored; they flower from midsummer onwards.

Hardy types can be sown outdoors in spring; some of these can be sown in early fall, to flower in spring or early summer the following year.

In cold areas such fall-sown annuals will survive better if protected by a cold frame. They can be sown directly into it and thinned, or sown in seed-trays and pricked out.

Soil preparation

Most annuals prefer sun, and medium to light soil. It should be dug 1 spade deep and rotted organic matter mixed with it at about 4½kg per sq m (10lb per sq yd). This can be done a month or so in advance, and then about 7 days before sowing or planting, rake in a general compound fertilizer at the manufacturer's recommended rates.

Before planting, the soil should be raked and cross-raked to produce a fine crumbly surface, level and evenly firm, and without weeds, large stones, large lumps of soil or other debris.

Annuals and biennials form a very large group of flowering plants; space permits only a very small selection here. The selection is, however, representative – including the most popular types and those which most effectively demonstrate the problems and methods involved in the growing of short-lived plants.

Growing annuals

Sowing seed

Seed can be sown in rows or in patches, fairly thinly, and covered with fine soil 3-6mm (⅛-¼in) deep, and watered in if no rain is likely within a few hours. Thin the seedlings first when large enough to handle, to about 5cm (2in) apart, and then when touching again, to their final spacing of about 10-15cm (4-6in).

Planting out

If fall-sown annuals have been over-wintered in frames, the small plants can be transplanted in early–mid spring. They will 'take' better if planted during the evening, and should be watered as soon as planted.

Thereafter keep the weeds under control while the plants grow and fill in the gaps, and keep supplied with water in dry weather. Some of the taller kinds may need small stakes.

Half-hardy annuals

Some annuals are not hardy – they are called half-hardy annuals (HHA), and they have to be sown indoors, in a temperature of about 16-18°C (60-65°F), in early spring. Then they are pricked out into 7.5cm (3in) deep seed trays,

spaced 5cm (2in) apart each way, when large enough to handle. Seed compost and a good potting compost should be used for each stage.

They are kept in these warm temperatures until the beginning of late spring, and then prepared for lower temperatures by placing them in a cold frame, and gradually giving them more and more ventilation by day and night. At the end of late spring or in early summer, they are planted outdoors, to flower from midsummer.

If gardens are warm and sheltered, sowing can be done in late winter, and the plants put out early in late spring, but be prepared to protect them at night from unexpected cold.

If the soil is rather dry, it should be watered with a fine spray before sowing. Where the seed is to be sown in lines, the rows can be lined with moist peat as well.

Begonia
Bedding plants, perennial in mild climates

Groups	**tuberous,** large-flowered, single or double, height and spread: 30-38cm (12-15 in), all colors but blue, midsummer-early fall; **fibrous,** small-flowered (semperflorens), single, 15-20cm (6-8in), pink, red, white, summer-fall; small flowered Lorraine types, as semperflorens kinds, but winter-flowering and for greenhouses only
Site/soil	sun or some shade, rich, moist soil
Soil preparation	dig 1 spade deep in spring, and mix in rotted organic matter
Sow/plant	start tubers during early spring in peat and gentle heat in greenhouse, pot in good compost, and plant out in early summer 23cm (9in) apart; plant fibrous-rooted kinds outdoors at the same time and with the same spacing
Cultivate	keep free of weeds and water well in dry weather; remove flower heads as they fade; lift tubers in fall, clean, and store dry in single layers in dark frostproof place for winter; discard fibrous-rooted kinds when flowering finishes
Increase	by seed sown in 20-25°C (68-75°F) in late winter-early spring; seed is extremely fine, and should be pressed into surface of very fine seed compost; keep at 16-18°C (60-65°F) after germination

Begonia semperflorens
The fibrous-rooted begonias produce many small, single flowers and have a long flowering season.

Troubles
Slugs and snails; aphids which spread virus – spray with bioresmethrin.

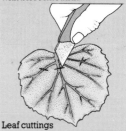

Leaf cuttings
Begonias with large, showy leaves can be propagated from leaves on which the veins have been cut.

Petunia

Half-hardy annual

Petunia
Petunias, although described as half-hardy, may flower into late fall in sheltered places.

Groups	much hybridized in recent years, there are now single and double-flowered kinds, some of the latter being carnation-like; also single-colored and bicolored (in stripes), large-flowered, and multiflora types, with smaller but very many flowers on each plant. Colors are white and all shades of pink, red, blue, purple; one or two yellow and orange hybrids are now also available; flowering time early summer-mid fall; height and spread: 7-38 × 15-30cm (3-15 × 6-12in)
Site/soil	sun, well-drained, moderately fertile soil
Soil preparation	dig 1 spade deep in spring and mix in rotted organic matter
Sow/plant	sow in warmth late winter-early spring, prick out when large enough to handle, and plant out after hardening-off in late spring-early summer
Cultivate	keep clear of weeds while small, water well in dry weather; remove tips of shoots to keep bushy; liquid-feed from late summer
Increase	by seed as above; by cuttings taken in spring
Troubles	slugs on young plants; severe weather can damage the flowers, but some varieties are tougher than others

Stem cuttings
Cuttings should be taken from young shoots about 10cm (4in) long. Cut the shoots close to soil level and trim them just below a joint. Put 2 or 3 cuttings into a 10cm (4in) pot containing compost. Put the cuttings into a frame, or cover the pot with polyethylene stretched over a wire frame.

Stocks

Hardy and half-hardy annual, biennial

Groups	**ten-week stocks,** height: 25-60cm (10-24in), mid-late summer; **East Lothian stocks,** 30cm (12in), midsummer-early fall; **Brompton stocks,** 45cm (18in), mid-late spring; these three have single and double flowers; **Virginian stock,** 23cm (9in), single, early-late summer; **night-scented stock,** 30cm (12in), single, summer. All are fragrant, pink, lilac, purple, red or white
Site/soil	sun for all; deep rich soil for ten-week stocks, well-drained medium-light soil for remainder
Soil preparation	dig 1 spade deep and mix in rotted organic matter generously for ten-week stocks, in moderate amounts for remainder, about 4 weeks before planting
Sow/plant	sow seed of ten-week and East Lothian stock in heat in early spring, and treat as half-hardy annuals; sow seed of Brompton stocks in cold frame in early summer and treat as biennials, overwintering in frame; sow seed of Virginian and night-scented stock outdoors in spring
Cultivate	discard seedlings of ten-week stocks with dark green leaves, more noticeable at a low temperature of 7-10°C (45-50°F), because these are singles; space 23-38cm (9-15in) apart, depending on final height; mulch after planting and remove seed-heads as the flowers fade

Stocks
Ten-week stocks are among the easiest of annuals to grow, and certainly the most fragrant.

Increase
By seed, as described opposite.

Troubles
Slugs attack young plants; club root; wilt – if the plant droops and the lower leaves turn yellow, destroy the plant and plant in new soil next year.

● Night scented stocks have fairly insignificant flowers and are best sown among other stocks – or under the windows for their evening fragrance.

Growing biennials

Another group of plants besides the annuals, which is grown from seed, is the biennial group. These are sown in late spring or summer, but do not flower in the same summer or fall. They produce shoots and leaves only at that time, and flower the next year, in spring or summer.

Foxgloves, Canterbury bells *(Campanula medium)*, some mulleins *(Verbascum)*, wallflowers, forget-me-nots and sweet williams, are all grown as biennials, though the last 3 can be short-lived perennials. Others grown as biennials are pansies, hollyhocks, double daisies and primulas, sometimes also the primroses, if colored, i.e. not yellow.

Soil and sowing

The soil is prepared in the same way as for the annuals, but sowing is done in late spring or early summer, in most cases.

Many can be sown where they are to flower and then thinned, but if space does not permit, they can be sown in a nursery bed or cold frame. Forget-me-nots and wallflowers do best if sown *in situ* in late midsummer, and thinned. Otherwise, the seedlings are pricked out into a nursery bed when 1 or 2 true leaves have appeared and transplanted during early-mid fall.

It is advisable to keep these small plants clear of leaves and weeds during winter, otherwise they get eaten by slugs, snails, springtails and woodlice or rot with constant damp.

The examples given on the next few pages are typical of plant grown as biennials in their soil, planting, sowing and cultivation requirements. Only wallflowers, however, are true biennials, the others being herbaceous perennials which are usually grown as biennials. This section, therefore, is more concerned with the ways of raising plants than with a self-contained group of types.

66

Antirrhinum (Snapdragon)

Herbaceous perennials

Groups	grown as biennials or half-hardy annuals; antirrhinums have been much hybridized, and are now available as dwarfs, heights: about 20cm (8in), semi-dwarf, 30-45cm (18-24in), and tall, 60-90cm (24-36in); flowers can be single or semi-double, like azaleas, hyacinth-, penstemon- or large-flowered as well as the normal antirrhinum flower; all colors but blue; antirrhinums have a very long flowering season which lasts from late spring until early fall – or until the first frosts; popularly known as snapdragons, because the mouth-like flowers can be opened and shut
Site/soil	sun, well-drained, slightly limy soil
Soil preparation	dig 1 spade deep and mix in organic matter, also grit if the soil is heavy, about a month before planting
Sow/plant	plant in mid spring 15, 30 or 45cm (6, 12 or 18in) apart according to height; sow as biennials and overwinter in cold frame, or treat as half-hardy annual
Cultivate	nip out main growing point soon after planting, to encourage bushiness; liquid-feed in light soil; support taller growing varieties with stakes
Troubles	rust fungus disease; use rust-resistant strains; spray Bordeaux mixture or dithane

Antirrhinum
Antirrhinums require very little attention after planting out and make ideal bedding plants.

Growing in containers
The dwarf and semi-dwarf varieties of antirrhinum can be grown quite easily in tubs and window boxes.

Hollyhock
Herbaceous perennial

Groups	usually grown as biennial, though annual kinds are now available, and plants can be left to become perennial; **tall,** height and spread: 180-240 × 45cm (72-96 × 18 in), single and double flowers, fringed and frilled; **medium height,** 135 × 30cm (54 × 12in), semi-double, fringed; **dwarf,** 60 × 30cm (24 × 12in), semi-double, fluffy flowers on bush-like plants.
Site/soil	sun, shelter from wind, medium loam
Soil preparation	dig at least 2 spades deep in late fall and mix in rotted organic matter generously
Sow/plant	sow outdoors in a sunny place in late spring or early summer, thin to 15cm (6in) apart in midsummer, and transplant in early fall, unless the garden is cold or the soil is heavy, then overwinter in a frame and plant in mid spring; plant so that crown is 5cm (2in) below soil level, and make hole deep enough to take roots vertically, not spread out or doubled up; sow annuals kinds in warmth in early spring, to flower from midsummer
Cultivate	mulch in late spring, keep well watered, and supply stakes
Increase	by seed as above; by cuttings of new growths produced in spring from parent plants and rooted in warmth

Hollyhock

The tall hollyhocks are the plants which characterize the 19th Century cottage garden.

Troubles
Rust fungus disease: use resistant strains and spray with Bordeaux mixture.

Watering
Keep the soil moist until the plants are well established.

Pansy
Herbaceous perennial

Groups	although perennial, pansies are usually grown as biennials. Summer-flowering (late spring and summer), include large-flowered kind such as the Roggli strain and the Chalon Giants, very large flowers with ruffled petals
Site/soil	shaded from the midday sun, well-drained fertile soil
Soil preparation	dig 2 spades deep and mix rotted organic matter into the top section, or bonemeal at 120g per sq m (4oz per sq yd); if the soil is heavy, mix in grit and lime to break it down
Sow/plant	for summer-flowering, sow seed in mid-late summer in boxes and put in a shaded frame; thin to 5cm (2in) apart and transplant young plants to permanent positions in early-mid fall, but if the soil is heavy or winters are severe, prick out and overwinter to plant in early-mid spring; space 30cm (12in) apart; for winter-flowering, sow seed in early summer, and move to flowering position in late summer or early fall.
Cultivate	apply a sandy topdressing mixture about a week after fall planting; keep small plants clear of leaves and debris during winter; remove flower buds from summer-flowering kinds until well rooted; mulch in late spring

Pansy
Although pansies are perennials, they are short-lived and are best used as bedding plants.

Increase
By seed, as described opposite; by stem cuttings put into outdoor shaded frames in late summer or early fall.

Troubles
Slugs attack young plants. Slug pellets are essential. All pansies and violas can be affected by a wilting disease which rots the crowns. Water seedlings and young plants with zineb or benomyl.

Wallflower

Biennial

Groups	**dwarfs,** height: 15-23cm (6-9in); **semi-dwarfs,** 30cm (12in); **tall,** 38-60cm (15-24in); some of the tall hybrids have large flowers; some kinds flower several weeks early; all colors but blue, chiefly in the yellow, orange, bronze and red range; fragrant; flowering time mid spring to the end of early summer
Site/soil	sun, well-drained slightly limy soil
Soil preparation	dig 1 spade deep in late summer and mix in rotted organic matter, also grit if the soil is heavy, and lime to correct any acidity
Sow/plant	sow thinly in late spring–early summer if possible where plants are to flower, and thin gradually to a spacing of 15-23cm (6-9in) each way; alternatively, sow in a seed-bed and thin to 15cm (6in) apart, then transplant in early–mid fall to permanent positions, planting firmly and watering in; pinch out the tips of the main shoots when plants are growing well; wallflowers dislike being moved
Cultivate	keep the seed-bed free of weeds; make sure transplanted plants do not run short of water; firm plants in if rocked by wind, and give a light dressing of a potash-high fertilizer in early spring
Increase	by seed as above

Wallflower
Wallflowers are among the best of spring bedding plants. They provide abundant color, often until midsummer.

Troubles
Club root is the only serious disease to affect wallflowers: soak planting holes with Terrador.

Pinching out
When the plants have been in their final position for a few weeks, pinch out the tips.

Growing bulbs and corms is comparatively easy. They grow well in light and fairly shallow soils. Indeed, sandy and other well-drained soils give the best results.

Amateur gardeners are often uncertain about the depth of planting: in general, plant bulbs with a covering of soil equal to twice their own depth.

Most bulbs will increase from year to year – a factor which makes spring flowering bulbs especially useful.

Growing bulbs

Bulbs and associated plants, such as corms and tubers, are a very special plant form, adapted in many cases to withstand considerable heat and drought in summer. The plant stores food in its swollen underground system, and this keeps it going until the weather becomes more amenable. Being underground it is buffered against intense heat or cold.

Many flower from mid winter until late spring, and then retreat, and ripen. Daffodils form embryo flowers in the bulb almost as soon as they finish flowering, and the leaves help to provide food for this to develop, until the dormant period. A few bulbs flower in summer, others flower after the summer heat in their native habitats and remain green through the winter.

Those that flower in winter and spring are in general planted some time in the fall, the earlier the better, as they start to produce new roots towards the end of summer, though no top growth will appear for several months. The fall-flowering kinds are put in during midsummer, the summer-flowering bulbs in spring. Sandy fertile soils give the best results, but bulbs grown in medium and heavy ones will flower well, provided the drainage is improved.

Anemone

(tuber, tuberous-like rhizome)

Groups	wood-anemone type, *A. apennina*, sky-blue, *A. blanda* and cultivars, blue, pink, rose-red, white, *A. nemorosa*, white, star-like flowers, spring; florist's anemone de Caen, single and St Brigid, double, all colors except orange, spring, summer, fall; these will generally flower 4 months after planting, except in winter if cold weather is severe
Site/soil	dappled shade, or full sun for some of the day; average soil for wood-anemones; well-drained and fertile for remainder
Soil preparation	improve drainage with grit if soil is heavy, mix in well-rotted organic matter for florist's anemones several weeks before planting
Plant	wood-anemones in fall 2.5cm (1in) deep, 7cm (3in) apart; others in early–late fall or any time from late winter–midsummer, 7cm (3in) deep and 15cm (6in) apart, best size is 2-3cm (¾-1¼in) diameter
Cultivate	maintain good supply of moisture at all times; keep free of weeds, protect florist's anemones with cloches in severe winter weather if top growth is present; give a general compound fertilizer as leaves start to grow again after dormancy period; dig up and divide every few years when dormant

Anemone
These plants have been known in European gardens for over 300 years.

Increase
From offsets, or by division of rhizomes at late summer – early fall

Protection
Anemone coronaria, which includes the florist's varieties, needs cloche protection during the winter months.

Dahlia
Herbaceous tuber

Groups	dahlias are classified for show purposes into many groups, according to flower shape and size; for the garden the best kinds are the **decorative** type, with broad, flat petals; the **cactus** type, with spiky, rolled-back petals, and the **pompom** or ball-shaped kinds, which are completely round and have tubular, blunt petals they are all colors but blue, height and spread: 23-120 × 30-90cm (9-48 × 12-36in), flowering midsummer-mid fall
Site/soil	sun, any soil, preferably moist and well-drained
Soil preparation	dig 1 spade deep and fork the soil below this; mix rotted organic matter into both levels; do this in winter or early spring; two weeks before planting, fork in a potash-high commercial fertilizer
Plant	plant stools (cut-down plants with tubers attached) in mid spring; plant rooted cuttings after hardening-off, in late spring/early summer; put in strong stakes before planting, at least 3 to a plant
Cultivate	tie to supports as they grow; thin out shoots and remove buds as required to produce larger flowers, except for short kinds; dig up after first frost, cut off top growth to within 15cm (6in) of tubers, clean tubers of soil and store stools in boxes in a frost-free place for the winter

Dahlia
Dahlias were cultivated by the Aztecs in Mexico for centuries before they were introduced to Europe.

Increase
Put stools in moist peat, and in gentle heat, in early spring. Take cuttings when shoots are 5 - 7cm (2-3in) long. Root in temperature of 18-21°C (65-70°F).

Troubles
Earwigs (*see Chrysanthemums*), aphids, capsid bugs: spray with bioresmethrin and dimethoate respectively.

Gladiolus

Corm

Groups	large-flowered hybrids, height: 60-120 cm (24-48 in), all colors, open flowers 10-20cm (4-8in) diameter, midsummer-mid fall; *primulinus*, 45-90cm (18-36in), all colors, hooded flowers 2.5-5 cm (1-2 in) diameter, similar flowering season; *colvillei* hybrids, tender, usually grown in cool greenhouses to flower spring–early summer, flowers small and widely open, height: 30-60cm (12-24in)
Site/soil	sun, sandy and fertile soil
Soil preparation	dig 1 spade deep, mix in plenty of rotted organic matter if sandy, mix in grit if heavy soil; prepare in winter
Sow/plant	plant corms every two weeks from the middle of early spring in sheltered gardens until late spring, plant 10 cm (4 in) deep and 15 cm (6 in) apart
Cultivate	supply 1 stake to the back of each plant when it can be seen on which side of the stem the flower-buds are developing; liquid-feed from this time on; dig up corms in late fall, dry in a frost-free shed, remove old withered corms, and store new ones singly in trays in a dark, frost-proof place for the winter
Increase	from bulbils at base of parent corm, these flower when 2 years old; by seed for flowers at 3 years

Gladiolus
Although hybrid gladioli are slightly tender, they are easy to grow and there are many varieties.

Small cormels which form around the main corm, can be planted separately.

Iris
Rhizomatous and bulbous perennials

Groups	**bearded iris,** *(rhizomatous)* height: 60-90 cm (24-36 in), all colors, some fragrant, early-midsummer; **English iris** (bulbous), *I. xiphioides* and hybrids, 30-60cm (12-24in), blue, lilac, purple, plum, white, midsummer
Site/soil	sun; well-drained, limy soil for bearded iris; moist and rich for English iris
Soil preparation	dig 1 spade deep, mix in grit if heavy, and lime to correct acidity
Sow/plant	plant bearded iris 30-45cm (12-18in) apart midsummer, mid fall or early spring, so that half rhizome shows above soil surface; plant English iris early-mid fall 7.5cm (3in) deep, 15cm (6in) apart, in groups for best effect
Cultivate	keep clear of weeds at all times; give superphosphate of lime in spring to bearded iris, 30g per sq m (1oz per sq yd); dig up every few years and replant
Increase	by division of rhizomes in 3rd year during midsummer; bulbs in 4th year by separating offsets and planting the largest, doing this in early mid fall, and replanting at once
Troubles	rhizome rot – rhizome becomes soft and unpleasant-smelling – dig up and destroy; iris borer, spray with Sevin

Iris
There are several hundred species of iris, most of them having a very long history.

Protection
If the rhizomes are exposed by frost, build up the soil to cover them again. Do not press the rhizomes down.

Lily
Bulb

Groups	the most easily grown garden lilies include *Lilium candidum,* height: 120-150cm (48-60in), white, midsummer; *L. regale,* 90-150cm (36-60in), white and rosy purple, midsummer; *L. tigrinum,* 120-150cm (48-60in), orange and hybrids, summer–early fall; *L. martagon,* 60-90cm (24-36in), pink-purple or wine, midsummer; *L. auratum,* 150-180cm (60-72in), white, yellow, red markings, flushed pink, late summer-fall
Site/soil	sun or a little shade, well-drained soil; *auratum* and *tigrinum* need acid soil
Soil preparation	fork leafmould into the top few cm (in), and mix grit into the lower soil if badly drained, in midsummer or early fall, depending on species
Sow/plant	plant *martagon* and the stem-rooting species such as *auratum, regale* and *tigrinum,* 15cm (6in) deep, and draw soil close to the stems of the latter group as they develop; plant *candidum* in late summer, the remainder in mid-late fall; cover the base of the planting hole with sand; avoid damage to the basal roots as far as possible
Cultivate	mulch annually in spring with leafmould; protect from frosts in late spring; keep supplied with water in dry weather; remove faded flowers to prevent seeds forming

Lily

Increase
By offsets, bulbils or scales: flowering in 2-4 years. By seed: flowering in 3-5 years.

Troubles
Virus disease carried by aphids – spray to control aphids. Buy certified bulbs and destroy at once any that are suspected of virus infection.
- Do not spread fresh manure around the roots – this may cause them to rot.
- Lilies that grow to more than 1m (3ft) should be staked.

Spring flowering bulbs

Groups	**large bulbs,** daffodil, hyacinth, narcissus, tulip, all colors, early spring-early summer; **small bulbs,** chionodoxa, crocus, grape-hyacinth, miniature daffodils, scilla, snowdrop; orange, blue, yellow, white, purple, mid winter–mid spring
Site/soil	sun for crocus, hyacinth, tulip, remainder sun or a little shade; well-drained soil
Soil preparation	mix in grit if soil is heavy; fork in general compound fertilizer one or two weeks before planting if soil is short of nutrient e.g. very sandy or stony
Plant	preferably early or mid fall; umn; tulips late fall if named varieities, not species; plant so as to cover bulbs with twice their depth of soil, e.g. daffodils 15cm (6in) deep. If soil is heavy, sit bulbs on a little sand at the bottom of hole
Cultivate	remove flower-heads after blooming unless seed is required, allow leaves to die down naturally; give potash-high compound fertilizer on soil round plants when flowering has finished, water in if the weather is dry, as the embryos of next season's flowers are formed at this time. If flowering decreases after several years, dig up bulbs when fully dormant in summer, discard small specimens, and store remainder in cool dark place, except tulips which need hot dry conditions to finish ripening, until planting time

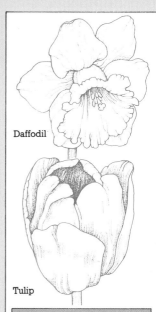

Daffodil

Tulip

Increase
From offsets, small bulbs produced at the side of parent bulb, separated and replanted in nursery bed. They flower in 2-3 years; from seed, in 3-5 years.

Troubles
Narcissus-bulb-fly caterpillars in bulbs: dust Sevin powder on soil around bulbs in mid and late spring. Bulb rot, eelworm and virus: no cure, destroy bulbs.

Growing shrubs

These woody deciduous and evergreen plants are among the most permanent plants in the garden. By choosing species carefully, it is possible to have a shrub in flower in the garden all year round, even in small gardens. The selection given here is far from complete, but it covers a wide range of types and requirements.

Shrubs need good soil preparation, digging 2 spades deep if the soil is deep enough, and adding rotted organic matter at the same time, at the same rates as those suggested for herbaceous plants. Medium to light soils should have 180g per sq m (6oz per sq yd) bonemeal forked in to the top few cm (in) a week before planting.

The roots should be given plenty of room; on no account should they be cramped or doubled up. If a support is needed, this should be put in place in the hole before the plant.

After planting, spray evergreens overhead with water every evening if the weather is dry, until growing well. Protect all from north and east winds, or from cold weather.

Prune early summer-flowering shrubs immediately after they have flowered. Do this by cutting off the flowered shoots, back to a strong new shoot which is suitably placed. The new shoots thus encouraged will be the ones carrying flowers the following summer. Prune winter and spring-flowering also as soon as flowering finishes; winter-flowering kinds, however, can often be left unpruned, except to tidy occasionally.

Broom
Deciduous shrub

Groups	*Cytisus* species and forms, include Common Broom, *C. scoparius*, height: 1.5-3m (5-10ft), yellow, late spring, and cultivars crimson, cream, bronze; *Genista* species, include Mount Etna Broom, *G. aethnensis*, height and spread: 3.6 × 3m (12 × 10ft), yellow, midsummer, and *Spartium junceum,* Spanish Broom, 1.5 × 1.2m (5 × 4 ft), yellow, summer
Site/soil	sun, well-drained light soil, acid to slightly limy; Spanish Broom will grow in chalky soil
Soil preparation	dig 1 spade deep and add organic matter only if very poor and dry
Plant	cytisus kinds fall, others fall–spring
Cultivate	no particular cultivation is required
Prune	cut cytisus and genista back immediately flowering has finished, so as to remove flowered shoots, cut to just above a strong new shoot; cut Spanish Broom back in mid spring, so as to remove at least half of each shoot produced the previous season; do not cut shoots older than this
Increase	by heel cuttings in mid-late summer
Troubles	occasionally aphids

Broom
Broom is ideal for giving quantities of color in spring.

Pruning
Cytisus and genista types require only the removal of the flowering shoots after flowering. This is done to produce bushy growth.

Heather
Evergreen sub-shrub

Groups	heather (*Erica* spp.), height and spread: 12.5-38 × 25-45cm (5-15 × 10-18in), and cultivars in shades of pink, purple, red, white, single and double; *E. carnea* kinds winter-flowering, *E. cinerea* summer–fall; heather or ling, (*Calluna* spp), similar heights and colors to ericas, red, also many with foliage coloured orange, red, yellow, grey, bronze, summer–late autumn; tree heaths, *Erica arborea*, 150 × 150cm (60 × 60in), white, spring
Site/soil	sun, or a little shade, well-drained acid soil; *E. carnea* and cultivars will grow on slightly limy soil
Soil preparation	dig 1 spade deep and mix in peat or leafmould
Plant	fall or spring; plant in groups for best effects
Cultivate	mulch in early spring with peat
Prune	clip over with shears just before growth starts to remove faded flowers; do this every year for callunas, every other year for ericas
Increase	by heel cuttings in late summer; by layering or division in spring
Troubles	occasionally wilt, a soil-borne fungus disease; dig up plants and destroy

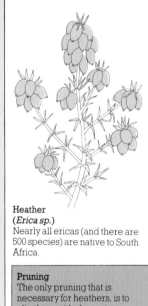

Heather
(*Erica sp.*)
Nearly all ericas (and there are 500 species) are native to South Africa.

Pruning
The only pruning that is necessary for heathers, is to clip them with shears to remove dead flowers. This should be done before the growing season.

Hydrangea
Deciduous shrub

Groups	**mop-heads,** have round heads of flowers (Hortensia group), height and spread: 60-150 × 75-120cm (24-60 × 30-48in); many cultivars in blue, pink, red, purple, and white; midsummer–mid fall; **lacecaps,** have flat heads of flowers, outer flowers different color to inner ones, 75-150 × 75-210cm (30-60 × 30-84in), similar colors and flowering time
Site/soil	sun or a little shade, sheltered from cold wind, most soils, good for coastal gardens
Soil preparation	dig 2 spades deep and mix in rotted organic matter
Plant	late fall-spring
Cultivate	keep well-watered in dry weather; mulch annually in late spring; blue flowers occur naturally in acid soil, pink/red ones in limy ones; for blue flowers on limy soil, water the plants with a solution of aluminum sulphate and iron sulphate; mix 7g (¼oz) of each with 4.5 litres (1 gal) soft water, leave to stand a few hours and then give each plant 9 litres (2 gal) weekly until flowering time, and once more in early fall
Prune	early–mid spring, by cutting out some of the eldest shoots at soil-level, together with weak and crowded shoots; leave flower-heads on plants until spring to protect new flower-buds lower down

Hydrangea
The hydrangea shown here is the most popular kind, the mop-head. They are hardy only in mild climates.

Increase
By soft tip cuttings in warmth during spring; by tips of ripe new shoots in late summer in an unheated propagator.

Troubles
Capsid bugs: spray dimethoate. Chlorosis (yellowing leaves): water with chelated iron.

● In cool gardens, there are two species of hydrangea that may be successful: *H. paniculata* and *H. arborescens grandiflora.* Both will withstand cold but may need shelter.

Lavender

Evergrey shrub

Groups	**Old English lavender** (*Lavandula spica*). height and spread: 90 × 90cm (36 × 36in), is the commonly grown kind, and good cultivars of this are 'Twickel Purple', less fragrant, and 'Loddon Pink', pale pink flowers. **French lavender**, *L. stoechas*, 60 × 60cm (24 × 24in), has dark gray spikes and deep purple flowers on top, very aromatic. All flower midsummer
Site/soil	sun, shelter from cold wind, well-drained soil
Soil preparation	dig 2 spades deep, mix in a moderate quantity of rotted organic matter, and add grit if the soil is heavy
Plant	mid fall or mid spring
Cultivate	keep well watered if weather dry immediately after planting; protect in severe winter weather; harvest flowers for drying just as they start to open
Prune	early-mid spring by cutting last season's new shoots by about half; do not cut shoots older than this
Increase	by half-ripe cuttings about 7.5cm (3in) long in mid-late summer, put in unheated propagator or pots with plastic covers
Troubles	leaf-spot fungus disease (dark brown spots); pick off affected leaves at once

Lavender
Lavender can find a place in almost any kind of garden – especially for its fragrance.

Lavender in tubs
Lavender will grow well in large tubs, but make sure that the root ball is moist when planted and firm-in well.

Rhododendrons & Azaleas

Deciduous and evergreen shrubs

Groups	There are very many botanical divisions and sub-divisions of rhododendrons, of which the azaleas form one. As far as the gardener is concerned, it is only necessary to understand that size range is from prostrate alpine shrublets to trees 9m (30ft) tall; all colors and shades of color are represented and flowering time is mainly late spring–early fall. Some rhododendrons and azaleas are not hardy
Site/soil	dappled shade, acid well-drained soil
Soil preparation	dig 2 spades deep and mix in peat or leafmould
Plant	fall or early-mid spring; plant root-ball complete without removing soil or spreading out roots; plant firmly and mulch with peat or leafmould
Cultivate	mulch in late spring annually with well-rotted organic matter (not exhausted mushroom compost which often has chalk in it); remove flower-heads immediately after flowering
Increase	by layering in spring or summer
Troubles	buds turn brown, killed by frost; bud blast due to fungus disease – buds turn brown also but become covered with black hairs – remove, and spray plants in midsummer with bioresmethrin

Rhododendron
There are a great many rhododendron species, most of them originating in the Himalayas.

Azalea
Unlike most rhododendrons, most azaleas are deciduous. They are, however, of the genus *Rhododendron*.

Roses
Deciduous shrubs and climbers

Groups	**large-flowered** (hybrid-tea type) height and spread: 60-150 × 60-120cm (24-60 × 24-48in); **cluster-flowered** (floribunda types), 60-180×60-120cm (24-72×24-48in); **polyanthas,** 45-60 × 60cm (18-24 × 48in); **miniatures,** 15-45 × 10-30cm (6-18 × 4-12in); **modern and old climbing** and **rambling roses,** mostly 3-4.5m (10-15ft), but some 9m (30ft) and more; the **Old Garden** roses, which include the old shrub cultivars, 90-210 × 75-150cm (36-84 × 30-60 in). Again, all colors but blue, flowering early–midsummer and some again in fall, some also intermittently from midsummer until mid-fall
Site/soil	sun or a little shade, shelter from north or east wind, most soils, preferably well-drained and fertile, but not very heavy
Soil preparation	dig 2 spades deep and mix in rotted organic matter, also grit if the soil is heavy; a few days before planting fork bonemeal at 120g per sq m (4oz per sq yd) into the top 23cm (9in)
Plant	mid fall-early spring; take particular care to spread the roots out to their fullest extent, and make sure the union of rootstock and scion is above the soil level, otherwise the scion will root and the plant deteriorate

Hybrid-tea type
Roses have been cultivated for many centuries, but the hybrid-tea roses are relatively modern.

Pruning
Hybrid-tea (bush) roses and floribunda types can be pruned in early spring. The procedure for the *floribunda* types is the same as for hybrid-tea roses (*see next page*) but cut some of the older shoots to leave only a quarter of their length. Prune **ramblers** in early fall, cutting the current year's flowering shoots away completely.

Roses
continued

Cutting back	cut the large-flowered kinds back to leave 10cm (4in) or so of stem, and the cluster-flowered to 15cm (6in) the stems at the top of standards should also be pruned hard after planting, to leave 4 or 5 buds on each. Ramblers should be reduced to 60-90cm (24-36in), if this has not already been done by the grower, and climbers can be left unpruned. Both types should be attached to their supports. The remaining types need not be pruned after planting
Cultivate	feed with a proprietary rose fertilizer in early–mid spring all those in the groups large and cluster-flowered, including standards, and polyanthas, and give another dressing in midsummer; mulch in late spring with rotted organic matter; remove dead blooms as they occur unless wanted for hips or seeds
Prune	pruning requirements for the different groups are given in the right hand column
Increase	by budding in midsummer, by ripe cuttings in mid fall; by seed stratified in winter and sown in late winter–early spring
Troubles	black spot on leaves, spray captan; mildew, spray benomyl; leaf-cutting bees, and cockchafer beetles eating flowers and buds, no remedy

PRUNING ROSES

Pruning bush/standard roses
Cut out completely weak, diseased, damaged and dead shoots and those growing into the center of the plant. Cut the remainder back by about half.

Pruning climbing roses
Prune in early spring by cutting sideshoots back to about 10-15cm (4-6in), and removing dead growth, old shoots and the tips of the main shoot.

The general instructions on this page can be applied to the majority of climbing plants. The examples which follow are designed to show how three completely different climbers are grown. But, because most climbers are shrubs, the information in the preceding section will also apply here. Sweet peas are exceptional in this respect, being annuals.

Growing climbing plants

The majority of climbing plants are woody shrubs which have taken on a specialized growth habit to enable them to reach the light and thus survive in crowded conditions in their natural home. It is therefore a good idea to provide ground-cover plants over the area where the roots run, to ensure coolness and moisture, especially for clematis.

The same provisions for soil preparation and planting apply as for shrubs, but, of course, supports are essential. Some climbers can be directed up trees or dead tree strumps, and allowed to grow naturally, without pruning.

Others can cover arches and pergolas, or be trained to furnish a house wall. The latter generally need trellis firmly attached to the wall, or a network of wires and wall-nails, to which the stems are tied with plastic-coated wire.

Some climbers are self-clinging, such as ivy, Virginia creeper and the climbing hydrangea.

Little pruning is required for most climbers, and is mainly to restrict them to the space available, and to remove the oldest stems. One or two, such as wisteria, rambler rose and clematis, flower better for regular pruning.

Clematis
Climber, deciduous or evergreen

Groups	large-flowered hybrids, height: 3-4½m (10-15ft), purple, blue, red, pink, white and shades of these, early summer, mid-late summer; species, such as *C. montana,* 10.5m (35ft), white, mid-late spring, *C. armandii,* evergreen, 4.5-6m (15-20ft), white, mid spring, *C. alpina,* 2.5m (8ft), blue and white, mid-late spring, Orange peel clematis *(C. orientalis),* 6m (20ft), yellow, late summer-early fall
Site/soil	sun or a little shade, average-heavy soil, well drained and slightly limy
Soil preparation	dig 2 spades deep and mix in generous amounts of rotted organic matter, particularly if on the light side
Plant	fall-spring; cut stem back to 15-30 cm (6-12in) when buds begin to swell, and support stem with small cane until it reaches main support
Cultivate	mulch annually in late spring; provide a cool root-run by ground-cover planting; keep well-watered in dry weather
Prune	cut back large-flowered, mid-late summer flowering kinds in late winter, cut hard to within 90cm (3ft) of ground level; prune large-flowered, early summer-flowering kinds at same time, but only by removing dead growth and cutting live shoots back by about 30cm (12in)

Clematis

Increase
By layering 18-month old shoots between fall and spring

Troubles
Wilt on young plants: cut shoots down to stumps at ground level and spray stumps and soil with zineb.

Sweet pea
Annual climber

Groups	tall climbing plants to 240cm (96in) or more, many named hybrids, midsummer-mid-fall; semi-dwarf bushy types, height and spread: 90 × 45cm (36 × 18in) and dwarf types, 30-38 × 50-60cm (12-15 × 20-24in),both flower early summer-early fall; a variety of colors – all fragrant
Site/soil	sun, shelter from wind for tall types, well-drained deep soil
Soil preparation	dig 2 spades deep and mix plenty of rotted organic matter and a compound, slow acting fertilizer into both levels, a month before sowing or planting
Sow/plant	sow seed singly outdoors early–mid spring, spaced 15cm (6in) apart; alternatively sow seed singly in deep, 5cm (2in) pots in early fall and overwinter in a cold frame to plant in early spring
Cultivate	stop young plants just above 3rd pair of leaves; for tall types, allow two shoots to grow and train each up a 240cm (96in) cane; remove tendrils and sideshoots from leaf axils as they appear; note that flower stems also appear in leaf axils, so watch for buds on these; for dwarf types,allow to grow freely after stopping and supply bushy sticks or netting for support; keep well-watered, and liquid-feed from late summer; pick flowers frequently

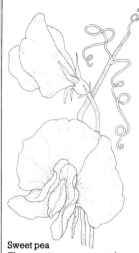

Sweet pea
The sweet pea season can be considerably lengthened by regular cutting of the blooms.

Troubles
Slugs may eat young shoots

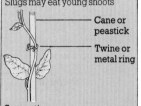

Cane or peastick

Twine or metal ring

Supporting
Sweet peas should be trained and supported by tying to canes or pea sticks.

Wisteria
Deciduous climber

Groups	*W. sinensis* is the species commonly grown, climbing 18m (58ft) and more if space is available, lilac flowers in late spring, and intermittently through summer
Site/soil	sun, rich, moist but well-drained soil
Soil preparation	dig at least 2 spades deep, and mix in generous quantities of rotted organic matter; fork in bonemeal a week before planting
Plant	in spring, spray top growth with water in late spring until leaves appear
Cultivate	mulch annually in mid spring, and again in fall if the soil is light; water well in dry weather; tie in new shoots as they grow
Prune	on wall-trained plants cut new shoots back in mid-late summer to just above 5th leaf from base of shoot, and prune again in mid winter to leave 2 or 3 dormant buds; alternatively, prune in summer to restrict the space available and tie shoots in evenly
Increase	by layering new shoots in late spring or summer
Troubles	lack of flowering, may be due to bird-pecking, lack of sun or lack of potassium – feed sulphate of potash at 30g per sq m (1oz per sq yd) in early spring

Wisteria
This is one of the most luxuriant of climbing plants and can be grown successfully against walls.

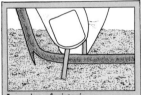

Layering of wisteria
Make a shallow cut in the underside of new shoots, cutting towards the growing tip. Bend the branch at the cut and peg to the ground with a wire hoop or staple. Stake the tip in an upright position and water-in.

There are, of course, many other aspects to ornamental gardening than the growing of flowers. Most of them are outside the scope of this book, but it is worth touching on some of the most popular and familiar elements of gardens. Trees, for example, are almost inseparable from gardens. Whether planted for their ornamental qualities, for shade or shelter, or simply left over from earlier use of the land, trees are significant features in almost every garden. Rock gardens and water gardens provide scope for more specialized interests. Wildlife and ecology enthusiasts will find ponds and pools very rewarding, and the creation of a rock garden will greatly extend the possibilities for growing ericaceous and alpine plants.

Rock garden plants

The needs of many rock garden or alpine plants are not great, once they have been planted and established. Grit, gravel or stone chippings on the soil surface round the plants, as a kind of mulch, helps to prevent crown rot, and rot of the lower leaves.

Dead-heading is advisable, and some of the creeping kinds need regular clipping back after flowering. Weeds must be kept strictly out of bounds because, once perennial weeds get into a rock garden, it is impossible to get rid of them completely. They insert themselves under rocks and invade from an impregnable base.

Likewise leaf removal in fall is advisable, to prevent smothering, and to remove protection for snails, slugs, woodlice and springtails. As the weather turns colder and wetter, grey or furry-leaved alpines will survive better with cloche protection.

Soil must, above all, be well-drained. Water-logging is instant death to most of the plants, more so than cold, which many are used to in their mountain habitats. If the soil is heavy, dig it out, and put in a drainage layer of rubble 15 cm (6 in) deep, then replace, mixed with copious quantities of coarse grit.

Water plants

Plants which grow directly in water rarely need encouragement in their cultivation but rather the opposite, so that their luxuriant growth is restricted and does not completely fill the pool or stream in which they are growing. Such cutting back needs to be done every few weeks during the spring and summer; at the same time weeds can be dealt with. Bulrushes and flags (irises) can become a great and persistent nuisance if not removed completely as soon as they take root.

Duckweed and blanket weed are other plagues of pools, whose only real control, if there are fish and other cultivated plants growing with them, is to drain the pool, clean it thoroughly, and start again.

Water plants are planted in late spring, just as their growth is beginning. They can be put direct into the pool bottom, or into baskets; covering the soil or compost with stones prevents it dispersing, or being dispersed by fish. Manure should not be mixed with the compost as it gives off substances detrimental to plants and fish as it decomposes. 'Greening' will disappear once the plants, fish, etc., have settled down to their feeding pattern.

Trees

No garden is complete without trees, but there is no need for it to be dominated by a towering species such as the white poplar of the plane tree, which are forest trees. There are plenty of smaller ones, 4.5-7.5m (15-25ft) tall, which will provide shade, height, and decoration in the shape of flowers, fruits and autumn leaf coloring (or evergreen leaves).

Trees are long-lived and the same care in soil preparation and planting as for shrubs and roses is necessary. A bad start, due to poor soil conditions, lack of nutrient, compacted roots and inadequate support, will result in a tree being weak and stunted all its life, if it survives at all.

Staking is essential for the first few years. Single or double stakes, put in vertically or at an angle, depending on the direction of the prevailing wind, should be rammed firmly into the hole before planning. Standards and half-standards are then attached in 3 places; just below the head, halfway down the trunk and near to ground level. This prevents wind-rocking , and the resulting hollow around the base of the trunk which fills up with water and eventually rots the bark.

ROCK PLANTS, TREES & WATER PLANTS

A selection of plants recommended for amateur gardeners

TREES

- Ornamental apple
  Malus species
- Bay
  Laurus nobilis
- Birch
  Betula pendula youngii
- Flowering cherry
  Prunus species
- Cornelian cherry
  Cornus mas
- *Cotoneaster hybridus pendulus*
- Hawthorn
  Crataegus species
- Judas tree
  Cercis siliquastrum
- Laburnam
- Maple
  Acer negundo variegata,
  A.n. elegantissimum
- Mountain ash
  Sorbus aucuparia
- Flowering peach
  Prunus species
- Whitebeam
  Sorbus aria
- Willow
  Salix purpurea pendula

WATER & WATERSIDE PLANTS

- Bog bean
  Menyanthes trifoliata
- Water forget-me-not
  Myosotis palustris
- Flowering rush
  Butomus umbellatus
- Water hawthorn
  Aponogeton distachyum
- Japanese iris †
  Iris kaempferi
- Kingcup †
  Caltha palustris
- Ligularia varieties †
- Monkey flower
  Mimulus luteus
- Pickerel weed
  Pontaderia cordata
- Water poppy
  Hydrocleys commersonii
- Primula †
  P. denticulata, japonica,
- Sweet flag
  Acorus calamus
- Waterlily
  Nymphaea species
- Yellow arum †
  Lysichitum americanum
- Yellow pond lily
  Nuphar luteum

† Waterside plant

ROCK PLANTS

- Alyssum
- Aubrieta
- Broom
  Cytisus kewensis,
  Genista lydia
- *Campanula muralis*
- Gentian
  Gentiana sino-ornata
- Houseleek
  Sempervivum tectorum,
  S. arachnoideum
- *Iris reticulata*
- Ornamental onion
  Allium spp.
- Pinks
  Dianthus varieties
- *Phlox subulata* varieties
- Rock rose
  Cistus obtusifolius
- Saxifrages
  (mossy and crusted)
- Stonecrop
  Sedum acre and others
- Sun rose
  Helianthemum alpestre and others
- Thrift
  Armeria maritima
- Thyme
  Thymus serpyllum

COMMON NAMES OF PLANTS
and their botanical equivalents

Agapanthus *Agapanthus orientalis*
Alyssum *Aurinia saxatilis*
Anemone, Japanese *Anemone x hybrida*
Astilbe *Astilbe* spp. & cvs.
Aubrieta *Aubrieta* hybrids
Bergamot *Monarda didyma*
Buddleia *Buddleia davidii*
Californian Lilac *Ceanothus* spp.
Camellia *Camellia japonica* & hybrids
Campanula *Campanula* spp.
Carnation, border *Dianthus caryophyllus* & hybrids
Catnip *Nepeta x faassenii*
Centaurea *Centaurea montana*
Christmas Rose *Helleborus niger*
Chrysanthemum, Korean *Chrysanthemum coreanum, C. rubellum* & hybrids
Clematis *Clematis* spp. cvs. & hybrids
Coreopsis *Coreopsis* spp. & cvs.
Cotoneaster *Cotoneaster* spp.
Crabapple *Malus* spp. & hybrids
Daffodil *Narcissus* spp.
Dahlia *Dahlia* hybrids
Day-lily *Hemerocallis* hybrids
Delphinium *Delphinium* hybrids
Deutzia *Deutzia* spp. & hybrids
Escallonia *Escallonia* spp. & hybrids
Evening Primrose *Oenothera* spp.
Forsythia *Forsythia* spp.

Gaillardia *Gaillardia* spp. & hybrids
Geranium *Geranium* spp.; *Pelargonium zonale*
Geum *Geum* spp. & hybrids
Gladiolus *Gladiolus* spp. & hybrids
Goldenrod *Solidago* hybrids
Heath *Erica* spp.
Heather *Calluna* spp. & hybrids
Hebe *Hebe* hybrids
Honeysuckle *Lonicera* spp.
Hydrangea *Hydrangea* spp. & hybrids
Hyacinth *Hyacinthus* hybrids
Iris, bearded *Iris germanica* & hybrids
Iris, English *Iris xiphioides* & hybrids
Japonica *Chaenomeles speciosa*
Jasmine, winter *Jasminum nudiflorum*
Jasmine, summer *Jasminum officinale*
Lavender *Lavandula* spp.
Leopard's Bane *Doronicum* spp.
Lilac *Syringa* spp. & cvs.
Lily *Lilium* spp.
Lily of the valley *Convallaria majalis*
London's Pride *Saxifraga x urbium*
Ling *Erica* spp.
Loosestrife *Lysimachia punctata*
Lungwort *Pulmonaria officinalis*
Lupin *Lupinus* spp. & hybrids
Mahonia *Mahonia japonica*

Mexican orange blossom *Choisya ternata*
Michaelmas daisy *Aster novii-belgii* cvs. & hybrids
Milfoil *Achillea millefolium*
Mullein *Verbascum* spp.
Musk Mallow *Malva moschata*
Old Man's Beard *Clematis* spp.
Onion, ornamental *Allium* spp.
Peony *Paeonia* spp.
Pentstemon *Pentstemon* spp.
Periwinkle *Vinca* spp.
Peruvian Lily *Alstroemeria ligtu*
Phlox *Phlox* spp.
Pink *Dianthus plumarius* and hybrids
Plantain Lily *Hosta* spp.
Potentilla *Potentilla fruticosa* and hybrids
Poppy *Papaver* spp.
Primula *Primula* spp.
Red-hot Poker *Kniphofia* spp.
Rhododendron *Rhododendron*
Rock Rose *Cistus* spp.
Rudbeckia *Rudbeckia* spp.
Salvia *Salvia* spp.
Scabious *Scabiosa* spp.
Sun Rose *Helianthemum* spp.
Sweet pea *Lathyrus odoratus* and hybrids
Syringa *Philadelphus* spp.
Tamarisk *Tamarix* spp.
Tulip *Tulipa* spp.
Veronica *Veronica* spp.
Wallflower *Cheiranthus cheiri* and hybrids
Wisteria *Wisteria* spp.
Witch-hazel *Hamamelis mollis*

Index

Acknowledgments

The 'How To' Book of Flowers and
Flower Gardening was created by
Simon Jennings and Company Limited.
We are grateful to the following
individuals and organizations
for their assistance in the
making of this book:

Lindsay Blow: *line and tone illustrations*
Pat Brindley: *all garden photographs*
John Couzins: *cover and title page photographs*
The Dover Archive: *engravings and embellishments*
Ann Hall: *compilation of index*
Peter Higgins: *photograph pages 6/7 top*
The Lindley Library: *bedding scheme pages 6/7*
Susan Milne: *color illustrations*
Van Withney-Johnson: *picture research*

Typesetting by Text Filmsetters Ltd., Orpington, Kent
Headline setting by Diagraphic Typesetting Ltd., London
Additional display setting by Facet Photosetting, London

Special thanks to Norman Ruffell and
the staff of Swaingrove Ltd., Bury St. Edmunds,
Suffolk, for the lithographic reproduction.